Baseball Bafflers

BASEBALL BAFFLERS

Quizzes, trivia, and Other Ballpark Challenges for the Hardball Know-It-All

EDITED BY FASTBALL MAKOV

BLACK DOG
& LEVENTHAL
PUBLISHERS

Compilation copyright © 2001 Sterling Publishing Company

This edition contains the text of the following original editions. They have been reorganized and reset for this volume. This edition was originally published in separate volumes under the titles:

Baseball Trivia Quiz Book © 2000 by David Brown and Mitch Williams
Baseball Brain Teasers © 1986 by Sterling Publishing Co., Inc.
Baseball's Strangest Moments © 1988 by Robert Oboski
Baseball's Zaniest Moments © 1988 by Robert Oboski
Baseball's Oddities © 1998 by Wayne Stewart
Baseball's Bafflers © 1999 by Wayne Stewart
Baseball's Funniest People © 1997 by Michael J. Pellowski
Test Your Baseball IQ © 1993 by Dom Forker

ISBN-13: 978-1-57912-167-9

Library of Congress Cataloging-in-Publication Data
Baseball Bafflers: quizzes, trivia & other ballpark challenges /
edited by Fastball Makov
     p. cm
ISBN 1-57012-167-5
1. Baseball-Miscellanea   I. Makov, Fastball, 1974
GV673 B.24 2001
796.357—dc21

Book and jacket design: Martin Lubin Graphic Design
Printed and bound in the U.S.A.

Published by

Black Dog & Leventhal Publishers Inc
151 West 19th Street
New York, NY 10011

Distributed by

Workman Publishing Company
225 Varick Street
New York, NY 10014

p o n m l k

CONTENTS

CONTENTS

Baseball, on the surface, is a very simple game. Beneath the surface, however, it is a very complex sport. The National Pastime has been played for 101 years—since 1900—in the modern era. Every play that has ever taken place on a major league diamond is covered in the rule book and its amendments. The umpires know the official rule book from cover to cover. Yet, new and unusual plays are constantly taking place, before they can be covered in the rule book, and umpires are still huddling with each other to interpret these new situations. If the official interpreters of the game can be stumped, it is not surprising that we, fans, reporters and followers of the sport, can be confused, too.

Some of the new twists that have come up include the following: 1) A non-pitcher who committed a balk without touching the ball 2) Four stolen bases on one pitch 3) A runner stealing first base, and 4) A batter-runner circling the bases in reverse order after a home run!

Would you anticipate such plays? Of course not. Does the umpire anticipate such plays? Again, the answer is no. But he has to be ready to react to them. He has to be informed. So should you. This book will teach you to be in the right position—as an umpire or a manager—to call these tricky plays.

Baseball, on the surface, is a very structured sport. Beneath the surface, however, as sports announcer Joe Garagiola has said, it can be a funny game. It's a game which has more than its share of oddities—of wild and interesting characters, of unusual plays, of crazy coincidences and witty quotes. You will find some of these humorous, sometimes bizarre, incidents in the following pages

Finally, the hardball trivia chapter will truly test your baseball I.Q. with everything from entertaining "Who said it?" match-ups to challenging "Who Am I?" quizzes.

Baseball Bafflers offers a look at the other side of the sport, the fun part that made us fall in love with this wonderful game in the first place. So, sit back, relax, and enjoy.

Baseball's Strangest Moments

MULHOLLAND'S MITT MAGIC

After watching baseball for decades, many fans come to believe that they've seen it all. In reality, the nature of baseball is such that just about the time you start to become blase, something odd will come along to make you shout, "Wow!"

One such play occurred on September 3, 1986, when a San Francisco Giants rookie pitcher named Terry Mulholland made an amazing fielding play. He was facing the New York Mets in the third inning when he stabbed a hard grounder off the bat of Keith Hernandez. It turned out the Mets All Star had drilled the ball so hard, it became lodged in Mulholland's glove. The southpaw hurler tried to pull the ball loose, but he also realized time was running out, and Hernandez would soon reach base safely. So, he trotted a few strides towards first base, gave up on freeing the ball, removed his glove (the ball still nestled inside), and tossed the glove to the first baseman, Bob Brenly. The umpire didn't miss a beat as he correctly ruled that Hernandez was out—in a truly bizarre play.

OPTICAL ILLUSION

During a 1969 game between the Atlanta Braves and the Houston Astros, a Houston base runner committed a terrible base running blunder. His mistake wasn't due to disobeying a coach, being outwitted by an opponent, or being unaware of the game situation. Instead, it was his own faulty eyesight that that duped him.

It began with the runner taking a normal lead off third base. As the pitcher began his delivery, the runner danced down the base paths a few steps. Then, upon seeing the ball bounce wildly off the mitt of Atlanta catcher Bob Didier, the daring runner darted home. It's hard to say who was more astonished a few seconds later, the runner or the catcher. But both men were clearly perplexed. The runner couldn't believe his eyes because there was Didier, still squatting at the plate with the ball in his mitt. Didier had certainly not missed the ball and was wondering why the runner would dash for a well-guarded home plate. Didier, however, was not so baffled that he didn't easily apply the tag for a ridiculously easy out.

MORE HUMILIATION

Max West was playing for the Boston Red Sox when he perpetrated a strange faux pas. It started innocently enough when West was retired at first base on a routine groundout. On the play, a teammate advanced to third base. West trudged back to his dugout, and he apparently was extremely slow in doing so. As he was about to descend the steps and make his way to the bench, he spied a baseball.

He probably assumed the ball had been fouled off by the next batter. So, as a friendly gesture, West stooped over, picked up the ball, and tossed it to the enemy catcher to save him a few steps.

But the ball had not been fouled off! It was in play, having escaped from the catcher after a pitch. In other words, it was a passed ball that would permit the runner off third to score. And, normally he would have scored with ease, but not when a teammate throws a perfect strike to the opposing catcher.

Needless to say, the runner was nailed at the plate. An official scorekeeper might even be tempted to teasingly give West an assist on the play. It's not quite certain what West's manager wanted to give him. But we can only imagine.

LOOPHOLE

Don Hoak of the Pittsburgh Pirates is said to have searched for, and actually found, a gaping loophole in baseball's record book. During a game in the 1960s, he reached second base. The next batter hit a long foul ball down the left-field line. Since Hoak couldn't be certain at first if the ball might drop in fair territory, he ran full speed for third base.

When the third base coach told him to hold up, that the ball was indeed foul, Hoak slowed down. He did not, however, retrace his steps back to second base, as is the normal procedure. Instead, he stayed in his tracks just a few steps away from third.

The umpire was puzzled and asked Hoak what he was doing. Hoak replied, "I'm taking my lead." There was no rule saying he had to return to second, and there certainly was no rule limiting the lead a runner could take off a base.

Therefore, the pitcher was given the ball and told to resume play. When the pitcher toed the rubber to get his sign for the next pitch, Hoak simply took a large stride and reached third base. Officially he was awarded a stolen base. Unofficially, he could joke with teammates about the great jump he got. Finally, a rule was devised to prohibit such tactics ever again.

Hoak's ingenuity was reminiscent of a Bill Veeck line.

Famous for taking advantage of any weakness in the rulebook, Veeck once proclaimed, "I try not to break the rules, but merely to test their elasticity."

BIZARRE BASE BURGLARY

Contrary to a widely held belief, Herman "Germany" Schaefer was not the first man to "steal" first base. Still, his story is such a classic it's worth repeating as a sort of Ripley's Believe-It-or-Not play. In 1911, while playing for the Washington Senators, Schaefer was on first base while a teammate, Clyde Milan, was taking his lead off third. On the next pitch, Schaefer took off for second, hoping to draw a throw from the catcher that might allow the runner from third to score. Instead of succeeding on this double steal, Schaefer was able to take second unimpeded, since the catcher offered no throw.

Undaunted, on the next pitch Schaefer scampered back to first base, and was again ignored by the catcher. That was fine with Schaefer, known to be the "clown prince" of baseball. In this case, however, he had more in mind that just foolery.

His plan was to retreat to that base in order to set up the double steal again. Of course, he wasn't officially credited with a steal of first, but it's said that he did rattle the pitcher.

So, on the very next pitch, Schaefer again streaked for second. For the second time in a matter of moments he stole that base. It's almost enough to lead to a facetious search of the record books for an entry; "Most times stealing the same base during one at bat, twice by Schaefer, 1911."

What's more, the runner from third finally did cross home in one of the game's most peculiar plays ever. Needless to say, nowadays there is a rule forbidding such an event. The rulebook bans such tactics, as it makes a "travesty of the game."

THE CASE OF THE DISAPPEARING BASEBALL

In 1958, Leon Wagner was a raw rookie for the San Francisco Giants. During a July game, the opposing Chicago Cubs took advantage of his inexperience. Cubs' batter Tony Taylor hit a shot to left field, where Wagner was positioned.

The ball bounded into the Cubs' bullpen before Wagner could track it down. He did notice, though, that the relief pitchers, who were viewing the game from that location, scattered. When those relievers stared under their bench, Wagner knew the ball had come to rest there.

He was wrong. He had been fooled by the enemy, who realized the ball had actually gone beyond the bullpen. In truth, the ball had come to a stop about 45 feet further down the foul line. It was nestled in a rain gutter. By the time Wagner understood he had been faked out, Taylor had breezed around the bases for one of the oddest inside-the-park homers ever.

DON'T ROLL THAT TARPAULIN COLEMAN MIGHT BE INSIDE!

Back in the old days, tarpaulins were spread out to cover baseball fields overnight and then rolled back manually by groundskeepers. Today, electrically operated tarps have become vogue. Push a button and it can be spread over the infield in a jiffy—push another button and it can be rolled back just as quickly.

One of the classiest of all powered retractable tarps is operated at St. Louis' Busch Stadium, and by sheer accident it became a cause célèbre during the 1985 League Championship Series between the Cardinals and Los Angeles Dodgers. Vince Coleman, the Cards' star outfielder and base stealing king, happened to be standing on the tarp along the first base side, casually warming up before the series fifth game, when a ground-crew member, not realizing anyone was still on the tarp, activated the rollup button. Within a second or two,

Coleman found himself trapped inside, being swallowed up as if a giant boa constrictor had wrapped its coils around him.

Coleman's screams brought out a rescue team, but not before some damage was done. His legs were so badly bruised that he could neither play in that fifth game, nor in the ensuing World Series that saw the Cardinals matched against the Kansas City Royals.

"The Coleman-tarpaulin episode certainly ranks as one of the strangest on-field accidents in baseball history," a St. Louis sportswriter commented.

"That tarp was a real man-eater," Coleman himself commented.

Sometimes when Busch Stadium is very quiet, one can almost hear faint murmuring from deep inside the tarpaulin machine, below the green artificial turf near first base. "Vince," the machine seems to gurgle, like the crocodile seeking the rest of Captain Hook in *Peter Pan*. "Vince, come a little closer to me, Vince."

Coleman, sensing that the tarp machine's appetite still may not be satiated since it tried to ingest him, runs faster than ever now—away from that "monster" machine.

TWO BALLS IN PLAY AT SAME TIME
AN UMPIRE'S MENTAL LAPSE

A college professor can be excused for being absent-minded, but not a big league umpire during the course of a ball game. Because Vic Delmore became absent-minded at a St. Louis Cardinals—Chicago

Cubs game played at Wrigley Field on June 30, 1959, he caused one of the strangest and most bizarre plays in baseball history.

The Cards' top hitter Stan Musial was at bat with a 3-1 count when the next pitch got away from Cub catcher Sammy Taylor and skidded toward the backstop.

Umpire Delmore called "Ball four" and Musial trotted toward first. But Taylor and pitcher Bob Anderson argued vehemently with the ump that it was a foul tip.

Since the ball was still in play, and Taylor had not chased it, Musial ran toward second. Fast-thinking third baseman Alvin Dark then raced to the backstop and retrieved the ball. Meanwhile, Delmore was still involved in the argument with the Cubs' battery mates when he unthinkingly pulled a second ball out of his pocket and handed it to catcher Taylor. Suddenly noticing Musial dashing for second, pitcher Anderson grabbed the new ball and threw to second—at the same time that Dark threw to shortstop Ernie Banks with the original ball!

Anderson's throw sailed over second base into center field. Musial saw the ball fly past his head, so—not realizing there were two balls in play—he took off for third only to run smack into Banks who tagged him out with the original ball.

After a lengthy conference, the umpires ruled that Musial was out since he was tagged with the original ball.

Also called "out" was Vic Delmore himself. Citing a "lack of confidence" in Vic, National League President Warren Giles fired him at season's end.

HIT A HOMER IN JAPAN
AND WIN A SWORD

Earl Averill, the Cleveland Indians hard-hitting center fielder, was a part of the delegation of American League All-Stars who traveled to the Orient in the fall of 1934 to play a series of 16 exhibition games against a team of Japan's top amateur and semi-professional players called the "All-Nippon Stars."

Averill's teammates included stars Babe Ruth and Lou Gehrig, sluggers Bing Miller, Charlie Gehringer and Jimmie Foxx, and pitchers Lefty Gomez and Earl Whitehill. The exhibitions were staged in cities throughout Japan, and by the time the series ended in late November the Americans had made a clean sweep by winning all 16 games.

One particular game between the Japanese and the Americans, played at Itatsu Stadium in Kokura, an industrial city on the island of Kyushu,

"May I honor you with this sword?"

revealed quite graphically the almost limitless enthusiasm the Japanese have for baseball. Rain fell the night before the game, which was scheduled for 2 p.m. on November 26, and the precipitation continued steadily as game time approached. The fans, however, didn't allow bad weather to prevent them from seeing a contest they had been eagerly anticipating, particularly since this was the only appearance the two teams would make in Kokura.

Hard-core baseball aficionados began lining up at the gates outside the park at 5 A.M. and when the gates opened around noon, some 11,000 persons had "bleacher" tickets. The catch was that there were no seats in the bleachers, which consisted only of the bare outfield turf. Unfortunately, the outfield was by then ankle deep in water, so the hardy bleacherites had to stand, kneel, or squat in the shallow lake for the entire game. (The total crowd reached 20,000 that day. Itatsu Stadium had only 9,000 permanent seats in addition to its "bleacher" capacity.) The fans in the outfield did not permit this minor inconvenience to dampen their enthusiasm for the big game, nor were they too disappointed when the All-Nippon Stars lost 8-1. They saw a well-played contest and, for the first time, got a chance to view close up the big American stars Babe Ruth and Lou Gehrig, about whom they'd read and heard so much.

One spectator, a middle-aged shopkeeper, walked 80 miles to see the game at Kokura, and he carried a sword which he vowed to give to the first American smashing a home run against the All-Nippon Stars. This valuable trophy was won by Earl Averill, who drove a long homer into the right field seats. It was the highest possible honor he could have received: Among the Japanese, a sword was not only a weapon, but also the warrior's badge of honor—it was thought to be his very soul.

When we spoke with Averill at Cooperstown's Hotel Otesaga in July 1981, just two years before his death, he recalled the 1934 Japanese tour and the game in Kokura. "That Japanese sword is the most unusual and prized trophy I ever received in baseball, and I've kept it in a glass case at my home in Snahomish [Washington] all these years," Avril said.

Averill hit 8 home runs on the 1934 exhibition series, while Babe Ruth paced the long ball parade with 13 homers. That trip to Japan marked Babe Ruth's last appearance in a New York Yankees uniform, incidentally, since in February 1935 he was handed his unconditional release.

GET THE X-RAY MACHINES READY!
NO CORK IN THE BATS, PLEASE!

In a mid-August 1987 game against the San Francisco Giants, New York Mets third baseman Howard Johnson poled a mighty home run at Shea Stadium, that allegedly measured about 480 feet. Roger Craig, the Giants manager, charged out of the dugout and told the umpires the bat should be impounded and turned over to league officials for examination.

"There's no way Howard Johnson could hit a ball that far without the bat being corked," Craig fumed.

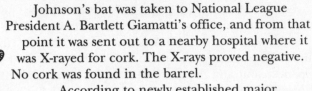

Johnson's bat was taken to National League President A. Bartlett Giamatti's office, and from that point it was sent out to a nearby hospital where it was X-rayed for cork. The X-rays proved negative. No cork was found in the barrel.

According to newly established major league rules, the manager of each team is allowed to challenge one bat during the course of a game. Since challenges are being registered in so many games, both the National and American League offices are considering buying their own X-ray machines in order to cut down on fees being paid to hospitals!

When cork is placed in the barrel of a bat, the batter is able to speed up his swing and hit for greater distances. Bats are supposed to be constructed of wood—and no other substance.

"Check that one again."

When manager Craig registered his protest, he noted that Johnson had never hit more than 12 homers in one season during his big league career before 1986 but he slammed more than 36 in 1987. He believed equipment tampering caused this phenomenon.

Ah, but Craig didn't realize that Johnson has been on well-planned weight and strength programs and had no need for corked bats in order to sock baseballs into orbit.

HIT ON HEAD BY BAT
WHILE IN ON-DECK CIRCLE

In 1945, Mobile catcher Harry Chozen had hit safely in 33 consecutive games and was on his way to setting a new Southern Association record of hitting safely in 49 consecutive games. Then, while kneeling in the on-deck circle, he was hit on the head and knocked unconscious by a flying bat that slipped from the hands of teammate Pete Thomassie as he followed through on a vicious swing. Chozen was forced to retire from the game.

After this episode, Chozen proceeded to hit safely in 16 additional games before being stopped. Southern Association President Billy Evans was called upon to rule, and decided that Chozen's failure to get a hit in that July 6 game, where he had walked in his only time at bat before being knocked out, did not break the hitting streak. The record Chozen broke stood for 20 years.

Chozen's record is interesting in several other ways. Twice during the streak he was used as a pinch hitter and delivered. On two other occasions, he entered the game in late innings, batting only once in each game, but he still managed to get his base hit. He broke the previous record of 46 in a truly dramatic manner by smashing a long home run in his first at bat in his forty-seventh game. (Chozen's only big league experience came in 1937 at the age of 22, when he caught one game for the Cincinnati Reds. He had a single in four trips to the plate.)

However, during an August 1978 game, Los Angeles Dodgers catcher Steve Yeager wasn't quite as lucky as Chozen in a batting circle accident. A Dodgers hitter broke his bat on a pitch causing a jagged piece of ash to sail straight for Yeager's throat. The team's trainer and doctor worked with lightning speed to remove the splintered wood from the jugular vein area. Yeager might otherwise have choked and bled to death. But after a couple of weeks on the disabled list, Yeager was back in action.

CENTER FIELDER CARLISLE MAKES UNASSISTED TRIPLE PLAY

The unassisted triple play is one of the rarest plays in baseball, with only 8 having occurred in the major leagues, and only a handful in the minors.

But Walter Carlisle, a center fielder for the L.A.-based Vernon team, on July 19, 1911, in a game against the Los Angeles Angels, executed perhaps the most spectacular unassisted triple play in professional baseball history.

With the score tied in the ninth inning, Charles Moore and George Metzger of the Angels walked. Pitcher Al Carson of Vernon was replaced by Harry Stewart. The Angels' third baseman, Roy Akin, connected on Stewart's first pitch for a low line drive over second base for what appeared to be a clean single. Moore from second and Metzger from first were off running on a hit-and-run signal.

Carlisle, playing in close behind second, lunged forward and caught the liner just off the turf, ending with a somersault, landing on his feet (he had been a circus acrobat). He raced to second base and touched the bag, while Moore was well on his way to the plate. Then he trotted to first, touching the bag to retire Metzger, who was still well past second.

Carlisle's name is secure in the record books, since he is the only outfielder to have pulled off the unassisted triple play. (Tris Speaker, the Hall of Fame center fielder active in the majors 1907–28, mostly with the Boston Red Sox and Cleveland, usually played in close and made several unassisted double plays. But Speaker never came close to running off the solo triple play.)

In recognition of Carlisle's singular achievement, the Vernon and Los Angeles fans presented him with a diamond-studded gold medal.

CRAMER AND WILLIAMS: A CLASSIC COLLISION IN THE OUTFIELD

When this writer was still in primary school, he saw one of his first big league games ever at Cleveland's Municipal Stadium on Sunday, June 23, 1940, as the Indians faced the Boston Red Sox.

In the eighth inning, Cleveland second baseman Ray Mack lined a drive deep into the left center field gap, with center fielder Doc Cramer and left fielder Ted Williams converging on the ball. In their mad dash they didn't see each other, collided head-on, and were both knocked unconscious as the ball rolled to the gate at the 463-foot sign. Mack got an easy inside-the-park homer.

Cramer was the first to get up, and after getting a whiff of smelling salts from the trainer, he was able to continue on in the game. But poor Ted Williams was carried off the field on a stretcher, and taken to a local hospital to have his fractured jaw repaired. "Ted the Kid" remained hospitalized for a couple of days and missed more than a week's worth of action.

It was always my impression that the collision was Cramer's fault because he was a 12-year big league veteran and should have directed the play on Mack's drive, while Williams was only a 22-year-old sophomore in the league.

We finally got our chance to question Williams about the play 47 years after it happened, at the 1987 Hall of Fame Induction Ceremonies at Cooperstown. Williams said: "Hell no, don't blame that collision on Cramer, it was my fault. I took off like crazy after Mack's liner and ran into Doc … if I left him alone, he would have had a good chance to flag it down. From that day on, I tried to look where I was going in the outfield."

PIERSALL CLUBS 100TH HOMER, RUNS THE BASES BACKWARDS

When Jimmy Piersall, one of the most uninhibited spirits in baseball history, slammed out his 100th major league homer while playing for the Washington Senators in 1963, he celebrated the occasion by running the bases backwards and sliding into home plate. Piersall probably thought at the time that this was going to be his last big home run—actually he managed to hit four more before he retired in 1967. Anyway, the league ruled that running the wrong way was illegal thereafter.

THE STRANGE CASE OF PETE GRAY, ONE-ARMED OUTFIELDER

Good ballplayers were extremely scarce during World War II, and the public, as well as the government, wanted baseball to carry on. The result was that many of the big leaguers of the 1942–45 period were those who were too young for the draft, or were classified 4-F (not physically fit for military duty).

The most famous 4-F of them all was one-armed outfielder Pete Gray, who had batted a solid .333 and had 68 stolen bases for the Memphis Chicks in 1944, achievements that won him election as the Southern Association's Most Valuable Player. Gray became the talk of the big league world because his play in the S.A. was so impressive.

The lowliest team, the St. Louis Browns, eagerly signed him for the 1945 campaign.

Gray had lost his right arm at the bicep in a boyhood accident, but he developed his left arm to such a degree and compensated for his handicap with such quickness that he became a really solid ballplayer. Gray had started out as a sandlot player in the Nanticoke, Pennsylvania, area as a teenager, and landed his first professional contract with Three Rivers, Ontario, of the Canadian-American League in 1942, at the age of 25. From that point, he moved up the minor league ladder rapidly.

This writer saw Gray in action several times with the Browns in 1945, and vividly recalls his performance against the Indians at Cleveland's Municipal Stadium in one particular four-game series in early June. Gray cracked out 7 hits, including a triple and a double— both hard-hit line drives to deep leftcenter—in 17 at-bats. Moreover, he fielded his leftfield post flawlessly. After catching a fly ball, he would flip his glove under the stump of his right arm in a rapid-fire motion so that he could throw the ball with his bare left hand.

Gray batted only .218 in the tough American League competition. Amazingly enough, however, he struck out only 11 times in 234 official at-bats. When Gray took the field either in a minor league or major league park, no one ever did him any favors—he got along on his own grit. As a result, he became an inspiration, during and after the war, to the multitude of disabled U.S. war veterans.

Gray unfortunately found himself back in the minors once the war was over. He retired from active play after a season with Dallas of the Texas League in 1949.

"GOOFY" GOMEZ
STOPS PITCHING IN WORLD SERIES
TO WATCH PASSING AIRPLANE

Vernon "Lefty" Gomez, one of the most colorful players in big league history, anchored the New York Yankees pitching staff during the 1930s. He became a 20-game winner four times, and wound up with an imposing 189-102 career record. Moreover, he won six World Series games without a loss (a record), and went 3-1 in 1930s All-Star competition. He was elected to the Hall of Fame in 1972.

No matter how critical the situation became on the baseball field, Lefty never lost his sharp sense of humor, and because of his constant practical joking he became known as "El Goofo" or just plain "Goofy" Gomez.

Gomez's most memorable goof occurred during the second game of the 1936 World Series against the hard-hitting New York Giants at the Polo Grounds.

More than 50 years after this episode, Gomez remembered it well as he related:

"It was early in the game, I was a little wild and before I knew it, there were two runners on base. Suddenly I heard a plane flying over the ballpark—it was a big airliner—and I just stepped off the mound, forgot about the runners, the batter, the game and everything else. I stood there watching calmly, until the plane completely disappeared from sight.

"Sure, I kept 45,000 fans (as well as the players) waiting and everyone wondered why I stopped the game this way … some people thought I was just plain crazy. Well, I was a little tense and I wanted to ease the tension a bit. As I recall, I came out of that inning pretty well unscathed."

The Yankees went on to whip the Giants 18-4 as Gomez went the distance, walking 7 and striking out 8.

The mists of antiquity may have settled a bit on the details of that game, but Lefty Gomez will always be remembered as the player who stopped the World Series dead in its tracks to watch an airplane in flight.

YOGI BERRA STRIKES OUT THREE TIMES, "NOT NOWHERE" WILL HE PLAY LIKE THAT

Yogi Berra is one of the power hitters of yesteryear who almost always seemed to get his bat on the ball, and managed to keep his strikeouts down to an extremely low level.

When he came up with the Yankees at the tail end of the 1946 season, Berra indicated quite clearly through his performance in the seven games he played in that he wasn't going to let too many third strikes slip by him. During those games, he bashed 2 homers and struck out only once. From that point on, Berra, a lefthanded pull hitter who was built like a fireplug (he stood 5-feet-8 inches high and weighed a solid 190 pounds), enjoyed five full seasons where his homers exceeded his K's: 1950–28, 12; 1951–27, 20; 1952–30, 24; 1955–27, 20; and 1956–30, 29.

In nearly two decades of big league play (1946–65), covering 2,120 games, Yogi hit 358 homers against only 415 strikeouts. Moreover, in 14 World Series from 1947 to 1963, covering 75 games, Berra hammered 12 homers against only 17 strikeouts.

Berra didn't play at all in 1964 when he managed the pennant-winning Yankees. And, after he was fired for losing the World Series, he landed on his feet as a coach for the New York Mets in 1965.

The struggling Mets needed an extra catcher badly, and so, Berra, then 40, was pressed into service. Berra saw action in only four games before he threw in the towel. In one game, he struck out three times. Afterward he told reporters : "I never struck out three times in one game before: not in the big leagues, not in the minor leagues, not in the little leagues, not nowhere. Now it's time to quit for good."

If everyone in the big leagues today who struck out three times in one game would voluntarily retire himself, the playing ranks would be surely decimated.

GAME BORES MANAGER— LEAVES BENCH FOR HOT DOG

When Luke Appling was managing the Kansas City Athletics on an interim basis late in the 1967 season, he became so bored with the game that he went up behind the grandstand and ordered a hot dog and beer from a refreshment stand. He didn't come back down into the dugout until he had finished his repast. As a result, Appling, an easy-going Southerner, was not invited to manage the Athletics for the 1968 season.

Appling, Hall of Fame shortstop, who played 20 years for the Chicago White Sox (1930–50), remained in various coaching capacities, even after his Kansas City experience. He made baseball headlines in 1985, when at the age of 78, he slammed a home run into the leftfield stands at Washington, D.C.'s Robert F. Kennedy Stadium during an Old-Timers' Game.

In 1987, Appling was still listed as batting coach for the Atlanta Braves.

TURNER MANAGES HIS BRAVES FOR ONE DAY

There had been eccentric team owners before. But when the flamboyant advertising billboard and television tycoon, Robert Edward "Ted" Turner III, bought the Atlanta Braves in 1975, little did the world of baseball realize how strange the diamond game could become with a completely uninhibited owner running a major league franchise.

Turner was at his outrageous best during a special "Field Day" staged at Atlanta Stadium shortly after he took charge of the Braves. He got down on his hands and knees, and pushed a baseball with his nose from third base to home plate.

Also, in his earlier days as team owner, he was often the star attraction at home games, where his rooting from his private box

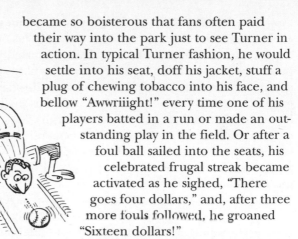

Ted Turner on Field Day

became so boisterous that fans often paid their way into the park just to see Turner in action. In typical Turner fashion, he would settle into his seat, doff his jacket, stuff a plug of chewing tobacco into his face, and bellow "Awwriiight!" every time one of his players batted in a run or made an outstanding play in the field. Or after a foul ball sailed into the seats, his celebrated frugal streak became activated as he sighed, "There goes four dollars," and, after three more fouls followed, he groaned "Sixteen dollars!"

Once his Braves became so deeply mired in the second division, that Turner threatened to call up his entire Savannah farm team to replace all of his Atlanta regulars.

Early in the 1977 season, Atlanta, under manager Dave Bristol, began floundering badly, and on May 10, the situation reached a climax when the Braves lost their 16th straight game. Turner could stand it no longer, so he ordered Bristol to go off on a 10-day "scouting trip" and appointed himself manager. On May 11, tempestuous Ted donned a uniform, ensconced himself in the dugout between two of his most trusted coaches (Eddie Haas and Vic Correll), and formally took over the reins as Braves pilot.

His players cringed at the sight of Turner in uniform because they knew his knowledge of the game's techniques was severely limited. For example, in his first days as owner, as his deputies explained the rudiments of baseball to him, Turner blurted, "What the hell is a bunt?" Despite the cringing and grumbling of his players, Turner called the shots for the entire game—with the assistance of his coaches—but he could do no better than Bristol as the Braves proceeded to lose their 17th straight game (to Pittsburgh) 2-1.

Most of the nation's baseball fans merely laughed off this moment of comic relief, and Turner felt himself ready to manage for a while longer. However, National League President Charles S. Feeney was not amused, and advised Turner that he was in violation of Major League Rule 20, which states in part: "No manager or player on a club shall directly or indirectly own stock or have any financial interest in the club by which he is employed except under an agreement approved by the commissioner..."

Commissioner Bowie Kuhn refused to give such approval, and Ted Turner's managerial career ended after a single game in the dugout.

In that 1977 season, Atlanta finished dead last in the National League's West Division with a dismal 61-101 record. However Turner is still officially listed in all the standard baseball record books as being manager for a day with an 0-1 record.

PITCHES FOR 23 TEAMS IN 13 LEAGUES
DURING A 27-YEAR CAREER

In an active baseball career that spanned 27 years (1924–50), Walter "Boom-Boom" Beck, a native of Decatur, Illinois, spent a good deal of his time traveling as he pitched for a total of 23 teams in 13 different leagues, including both major leagues. In addition to his American and National League experience, Beck toiled in the following circuits that are obscure to many fans: Three-I League, Texas Association, Western League, American Association, International League, Southern Association, Pacific Coast League, Inter-State League, Southeast League, Central League and Middle Atlantic League. (In the latter three leagues, he was a player-manager.)

As a major leaguer, the righthanded-throwing Beck saw action with the St. Louis Browns, Brooklyn Dodgers, Philadelphia Phillies, Detroit Tigers, Cincinnati Reds and Pittsburgh Pirates, and posted a 38-69 record in 265 games. In the minors, he went 199-167, making his total pro regular season record come to just one victory over .500, or 237-236.

Beck enjoyed his finest season in the minors with the Memphis Chicks in 1932, when he rolled up an impressive 27-6 mark to rank as the leading pitcher in the Southern Association. That earned him a return trip to the big leagues in 1933, this time with Brooklyn, and it was in Flatbush that Beck earned his unusual nickname.

While pitching against the Phillies on a sweltering 1934 afternoon in Philadelphia's Baker Bowl, Beck was removed from the game by manager Casey Stengel while still holding a slim lead. Losing his cool, Beck wound up and threw the ball with all his strength toward rightfield where it made a resounding "boom" as it struck the tin fence. Outfielder Hack Wilson, who had not been paying attention during the pitching change, heard the boom and, thinking the ball was in play, fielded it and made a perfect line throw to second base. This unusual episode caused all the fans and players, except for Beck, to laugh heartily. From that time on, Beck was known as "Boom-Boom." Wilson, a Hall of Famer, who had his best season in the majors with the Chicago Cubs when he hit 56 homers and knocked in 190 runs (the all-time major league record), was then in the twilight of his career and found himself released by the Dodgers. He signed with the Phillies later in the 1934 season.

After his playing days were over, "Boom-Boom" Beck remained in baseball for another two decades as a coach and scout at both the major and minor league levels. He died in Champaign, Illinois, on May 7, 1987, at the age of 82.

TY COBB: LONG BALL HITTER AND TIGER ON THE BASE PATHS

"Ty Cobb is absolutely the greatest ballplayer I've ever seen on the diamond, and that includes everyone I've either played with or against," declared Hall of Fame infielder, Joe Sewell, in an interview conducted in 1987 at Cooperstown's Hotel Otesaga.

Sewell went on to say:

"When not in uniform, Ty Cobb personified the true Southern gentleman, but once he put on the Detroit flannels, he seemed to change character, almost like a Jekyll and Hyde. He played every inning of every game as if it were the critical point of a World Series …. Even when he took his position in the outfield, he appeared like a tiger ready to spring.

"When he came roaring into second base on a close play, or to break up a double play, he reminded me of a runaway locomotive. He loudly proclaimed that the base line belonged to him, and felt justified in running over any infielder who got in his way. But anyone who saw me play knows I didn't bail out when Cobb barreled into second base. I gave him as much as he gave me."

No question about that because Sewell, who stood only 5 feet 7 inches and weighed 160 pounds, had the reputation of being a very scrappy and aggressive shortstop (later in his career he switched over to third base). He made up for his lack of size with his own special brand of ferocity.

In continuing to recall Cobb's exploits on the baseball diamond, Sewell said:

"When I played against Cobb in the 1920s, he was getting well on into his 30s, but age didn't stop him a bit from being a demon on the base paths. Remember that Cobb was never the fastest runner in baseball, not even when he came up to the Tigers as a kid in 1905. But he knew how to run because he studied how to stride properly … he learned to cut yards off the distance between bases by knowing how to make sharp turns and how to tag the bag on the inside. He ran in straight lines. How many times do you see players today making wide turns and running any number of unnecessary yards in circling the bases?

"Sure, I pick Ty Cobb as the greatest ballplayer of all time, even ahead of Babe Ruth," Sewell pontificated without a noticeable trace of doubt in his voice. "Remember that I played against Ruth during his peak years … and I was his teammate on the Yankees in the early 1930s when he was still going good. Ruth hit all those home runs, but Cobb could whack the ball as hard as anyone. I know firsthand because I caught lots of his drives that nearly broke my hand.

"The sportswriters began getting on Cobb in the mid-1920s because he was still content to hit singles and doubles when the home run was just coming into vogue. So he decided to show everyone he could match Ruth or anyone else for power. If I remember correctly, it was at St. Louis' Sportsman's Park in early May 1925 that Cobb decided to take a full swing and put on a real power exhibition. In the first game of the series, he went six for six and clubbed three homers, and on the next, he hammered two more homers—that was five in two days and enough to tie the major league record. As I recall, he got two doubles in those two games that nearly cleared the wall. He just missed seven homers in two days.

"Then Cobb went back to his natural snap swing batting style, but he proved his point that hitting home runs was no great trick," Sewell added.

JOE SEWELL:
"IRON MAN A TOUGH BATTER TO STRIKE OUT"

Joe Sewell broke into the big leagues under both tragic and dramatic circumstances. He was called up by the Cleveland Indians from the New Orleans Pelicans of the Southern Association on August 18, 1920. This was the day after their regular shortstop, Ray Chapman, was killed by a pitch thrown by the New York Yankees submarine artist Carl Mays at the Polo Grounds, New York. Chapman is the only player in major league history to have been killed during the course of a game.

Sewell stepped right into the shortstop slot and, with his timely hitting and good fielding, helped the Indians capture both the American League pennant and a World Series victory over the Brooklyn Dodgers.

Sewell remained with the Indians through 1930, playing mostly at shortstop, and then spent the final three years of his career with the New York Yankees as a third baseman. In 14 years of big league action, Sewell, a lefthanded hitter, banged out 2,226 base hits in 1,903 games and had a batting average of .312, a sound enough record to earn him Hall of Fame election in 1977.

Amazingly enough, Sewell struck out only 114 times in those 14 years, in over 8,000 total plate appearances (including walks, sacrifices, etc.). He whiffed but three times in both 1930 and 1932, and he struck out only four times in three other seasons—and all these were when he was a regular, playing in well over 100 games per year.

Sewell is the all-time big league champion in being the toughest man to strike out.

When we spoke with Sewell in July 1987 in Cooperstown, we asked him why so many of today's hitters are fanning so frequently, pointing out that some of them roll up 114 strikeouts even before the season winds into August.

"Because they don't keep their eye on the ball!" snapped the 89-year-old Sewell, who is still very much alert, sharp-tongued and sharp-minded. "Too many batters today swing wildly trying for the home run instead of just going with the pitch and meeting the ball. If you're talking about strange baseball, it's strange to me why so many contemporary players lack discipline and refuse to control their swings the way they should."

Sewell added:

"Don't forget that the pitchers I faced in the 1920s and 1930s were just as fast as the ones throwing today. I faced flame throwers like Walter Johnson and Lefty Grove, and they had a hard time striking me out because I had a compact swing and watched the ball the whole way. It's hard for me to imagine that legions of batters in the 1980s are striking out 125 to 150 times and more per season and not getting farmed out."

That may be because they have million-dollar contracts.

Sewell was an authentic "Iron Man" of his day, playing in 1,103 consecutive games from 1922 to 1928. At that time, Sewell's Iron Man performance ranked second only to that of Everett Scott, American League infielder who played in 1,307 games in a row from 1916 to

1925. Even now, Sewell's streak ranks as No. 5 on the all-time list. Lou Gehrig stands as No. 1, of course, with his staggering total of 2,130 straight games.

When asked why his streak finally came to a halt, Sewell replied: "One morning I got up and found out I had the flu real bad, and so I had to crawl right back into bed. Still, no one made a big fuss about playing streaks 50-60 years ago. At that time, my 1,103 straight games plus a dime would be good for a cup of coffee."

(Cal Ripken, Jr., Baltimore Orioles shortstop, established a big league record by playing 8,243 consecutive innings over the course of 908 games, but was pulled out in the eighth inning on a September 14, 1987 game by his father, manager Cal Ripken, Sr., who said: "I wanted to get everybody to stop writing about the consecutive inning streak. The media pressure on us was getting intense, and so we just had to put an end to the streak.")

Sewell also recalled: "Lifetime records didn't attract all that much attention in the old days. I remember when Tris Speaker, our manager and center fielder at Cleveland, got base hit Number 3,000 in 1925 … there was hardly a ripple about it. The newspapers made passing mention of this milestone, but 'Spoke' received nothing in the way of special tributes."

Accordingly, Clifford Kachline, former Hall of Fame Historian and longtime baseball writer, commented that Ty Cobb received relatively little publicity when he lined out base hit No. 4,000 while playing for the Philadelphia A's in 1927.

"Just check Cobb's file in the Hall of Fame Library and you won't see any banner headlines about that milestone," Kachline said.

Also, there's no record of the President in 1927 calling from the Oval Office in the White House to congratulate Cobb. When Pete Rose broke Stan Musial's National League base hit record of 3,630, Ronald Reagan got right on the White House phone to call Rose before Rose had a chance to take his post-game shower. And when Rose got hit Number 4,192 in 1985 to pass Ty Cobb on the all-time list, Mr. Reagan got on the White House phone again to congratulate Rose again.

"Everybody is statistics-happy today, even the President of the United States," muttered Sewell.

JIMMIE FOXX AND MICKEY MANTLE: WHO HIT THE BALL HARDER?

If Jimmie Foxx had stuck more closely to training rules, he could have piled up even more impressive statistics. Through the 1940 season, when Foxx was only 33, he had already smashed out an even 500 homers. From that point on, he was only able to hit 34 more in the big leagues.

Foxx stood an even 6 feet in height, weighed about 210 pounds, and was proportioned like Charles Atlas, with a massive chest and powerful forearms. Called "The Beast" because of his enormous strength (he developed his physique as a Maryland farm boy), he could hit homers righthanded as far as Babe Ruth could hit them lefthanded.

As a member of the Boston Red Sox in 1938, he lined a shot to the deepest corner of the leftfield bleachers at Cleveland's Municipal Stadium 435 feet away. Lots of hitters can blast baseballs 435 feet, but Foxx's line drive had so much velocity behind it that it broke the back of a wooden seat at that great distance!

On one occasion in batting practice, Foxx hit a drive back to the box with such force that the pitcher could not get his glove up in time to shield himself (as Mark Eichhorn was able to do), and suffered a fractured skull. The pitcher, a promising youngster, saw his career end on that fateful day.

Billy Martin once said Mickey Mantle could hit a baseball harder than anyone he ever saw ... that may be true, but Martin never saw Ruth and Foxx in action. In deference to Mantle, however, his greatest moment of glory in the power department came on May 30, 1955, at Griffith Stadium when he faced Washington's Pedro Ramos.

Mantle, a switch-hitter batting lefthanded, caught hold of one of Ramos' fastballs and propelled an immensely high drive that appeared to have enough power behind it to clear the rightfield roof, a feat that no player had accomplished in the stadium's half-century history. None of the great sluggers of baseball had even come close to powering a fair ball over the giant-sized filigree, the ornamental work hanging from the lip of the stands, which, in both rightfield and leftfield, hooks into fair territory toward the bleachers. Mantle hit the filigree, and as Joe Reichler, *Associated Press* baseball writer, who witnessed the drive, said: "He came so close to making history that he still made it. The ball struck high on the facade, barely a foot or two below the edge of the roof ... For years after that spring 1955 game, fans who came to Griffith Stadium lifted their eyes and stared at the spot where the ball hit. Likely many of them remembered the 565-foot homer Mantle hit in Washington two years before. Unobstructed, the drive against Ramos would have traveled even further."

WHAT RIGHTHANDED BATTER
LAST HIT .380 OR BETTER? JOE D. IN 1939

When Joe DiMaggio, New York Yankees center fielder, won the American League batting championship with a .381 average in 1939, he became the last righthanded hitter in the major leagues to hit .380 or better. Joe played in only 120 games in 1939 because he held out for more than a month at the beginning of the season. He finally settled for a contract calling for $30,000, a small fraction of what he could earn if he were playing today.

DON MATTINGLY:
HITS WITH EXTRA OOMPH,
SETS TWO HOMER RECORDS IN 1987

Don Mattingly has been noted primarily for his fielding and his high batting average. He smashes hard line drives to every part of the field, with home runs merely a secondary affair until 1987. In his first four seasons with the New York Yankees (1983–86) Mattingly, a 5-foot-11-inch 185 pound lefthanded swinger, belted a good, not great, 93 homers, while batting at a sizzling clip of .332.

In 1987, Mattingly continued his usual high batting average and modest home run-hitting pace. But, while hitting 30 homers, Mattingly, extraordinarily enough, was able to both tie and break two all-time major league home run records.

In July, he hit for the circuit in eight consecutive games, tying the major league mark established by Pittsburgh's Dale Long in 1956. Then on September 29 at Yankee Stadium against Boston, he whacked his sixth grand slam of the season, breaking the record of five that had been shared by Ernie Banks of the Chicago Cubs (1955) and Jim Gentile of the Baltimore Orioles (1961). Oddly, Mattingly had never hit a grand slammer before the 1987 season.

Mattingly's record-breaking sixth grand slam came in the third inning off Boston lefthander Bruce Hurst. The ball carried 11 rows into the third tier of the rightfield stands and powered the Yankees to a 6-0 victory over the Red Sox.

Mattingly had never hit Hurst well in the past, averaging a mere .217 with no homers.

When questioned by reporters after the game about his grand slam slugging splurge, Mattingly modestly replied, "I can't explain it. I basically haven't done anything different, other than to try to hit the ball hard. Before, I would hit a sacrifice fly with the bases loaded. Now, I think of hitting the ball hard. Consequently, if I get the ball in the air, it carries."

BOB BUHL GOES 0 FOR 70

In respect to all-time weak-hitting pitchers, Bob Buhl rates a top spot in that category. While with the Chicago Cubs and Milwaukee Braves in 1962, Buhl "distinguished" himself by going 0 for 70, winding up with a batting average of .000. No other player in major league history, pitcher or otherwise has gone to bat that many times in a season without a single bingle.

Buhl struck out about half the time; 36 K's were registered against him during that ignominious 0 for 70 streak at bat, though he did manage to walk six times, and score two runs.

Over the course of 15 years in the big leagues (1953–67), Buhl went 76 for 857, good for a .089 average, and somehow he managed two doubles, which brought his "slugging" average up to .091. He scored a grand total of 31 runs, drove in 26 and struck out 389 times.

As a pitcher, however, Buhl posted a very competent 166-132 for a .557 percentage, reaching his peak in 1957 for Milwaukee when he went 18-7 as he played a key role in helping the Braves capture the National League pennant. Buhl's record as a batsman literally cried out for the DH (Designated Hitter) rule.

DEL ENNIS LEAVES 500 STRANDED
CLEAN-UP HITTER CAN'T CLEAN UP

Del Ennis, a hard-hitting outfielder, came up with the Philadelphia Phillies in 1946, and reached his peak in 1950 when he helped the Phillies' so-called "Whiz Kids" to the National League pennant. Ennis compiled excellent stats that year—he hit 31 homers, drove in a league high 126 runs, and averaged .311 at bat.

However, a team of sportswriters for the *Philadelphia Inquirer* still felt that Ennis, hitting in the fourth position, wasn't driving in enough runs, particularly since the three batters who ordinarily preceded him in the order (Eddie Waitkus, Richie Ashburn and Willie "Puddin' Head" Jones), always seemed to be on base. The reporters went back and checked the results of every game, and discovered that Ennis left over 500 men on base during the course of the 1950 season.

"If that isn't a record for leaving men on, it sure comes close to it!" one of the writers declared. "If Ennis was a better clutch hitter—and with all those men he had on base—he could have easily broken Hack Wilson's major league record of 190 runs batted in for one season."

The Phillies experienced total disaster in the World Series that year as they were wiped out by the Yankees in four straight games. Ennis didn't help the cause much as he went 2 for 14 and failed to drive in a single run.

SENATORS, WITH WALTER JOHNSON' BIG LOSERS
BUT NOT THE WORST

The Washington Senators experienced their worst season in 1909 as they finished dead last under manager Joe Cantillon with a 42-110 record, for a lowly .276 percentage. The Senators wound up exactly 56 games behind the pennant-winning Detroit Tigers.

The Senators started the season poorly, but sagged even more in midseason. Of the 34 games played in July, they managed to lose 29. That still remains as the all-time record for the most games lost by one team in a month.

For the season, the great Walter Johnson, then in his third year in the majors, rolled up a dismal 13-25 won-lost record, while his fellow righthander, rookie Bob Groom, "fashioned" a 7-26 mark. No big league pitcher in the 20th century has lost more games in a season than Bob Groom.

Though they were big losers, Johnson and Groom could justifiably complain about weak hitting support since they posted glittering earned run averages of 2.21 and 2.87, respectively. In team batting, Washington finished last with a puny .223 mark.

Was this baseball's "worst" team? No. Other teams have actually experienced worse months. In August 1890, the National League Pittsburgh Pirates went 1-27, and the Cleveland Spiders tied that record in their final National League year in 1899, when they staggered to a 1-27 record for the month of September.

Pittsburgh for the entire 1890 season, wound up with a miserable 23-113 (.169 percentage), while the 1899 Cleveland Spiders finished with a horrendous 20-134 record (.149 percentage). No other major league team has surpassed this.

SHORTEST GAME IN PRO BALL—
9 INNINGS IN 32 MINUTES!

The average nine-inning major league game today requires about two hours and 45 minutes to complete. However, a game can be played much faster—as was proved by the Southern Association during an experiment conducted on September 19, 1910, which proved that 32 minutes is all you really need.

In this 32-minute game, Mobile edged the home team Atlanta Crackers 2-1. With the score tied 1-1 in the first half of the ninth, Mobile pushed across the decisive run. Both teams hustled every minute of the way. Batters did not wait out the pitchers, but rather swung at every good pitch. There was only one walk; not a single player struck out; and, Mobile even reeled off a triple play. Mobile made 6 hits against 4 for Atlanta. On the same afternoon, Chattanooga at Nashville in another Southern Association game, needed only 42 minutes to complete.

BASEBALL HALL OF FAME
HOUSES STRANGE SPECIMENS OF THE GAME

"Be careful how you hold this," Peter P. Clark, Baseball Hall of Fame Museum Registrar warned us as he handed over an artifact he pulled out of a cabinet in his lower-level museum office. We followed Clark's advice because this particular specimen of diamond game memorabilia turned out to be a Gillette razor blade taped onto a sheet of letter paper. The inscription was a note testifying to the fact that this blue blade was used by Cy Young on September 9, 1953, during a visit to a friend's house in East Cuyahoga Falls, Ohio.

The Cy Young razor blade is among numerous items in the Hall of Fame Museum collection not ordinarily placed on display. A razor blade in a baseball museum? Strange.

But that's not all. After Clark gingerly placed the Cy Young Gillette blade back into the cabinet, he hauled out a chunk of wood, measuring about 16 inches in length and some 6 inches thick. This solid-looking specimen of wood—more specifically red oak—was inscribed in pen as being the last block of wood cut with an axe by Cy Young, and dated November 8, 1954. Moreover, Cy Young, the 511-game winner, who spent his long retirement from baseball as a farmer in Newcomerstown, Ohio, autographed the chunk of oak soon after he chopped it. He was 87 at the time. (Young died on November 4, 1955, at the age of 88.)

"The Cy Young oak is a part of our permanent holdings, but one wonders what a collector would pay for it at public auction," mused Clark. "Almost any sort of artifact dealing with a Hall of Famer seems to have special appeal," he added.

Cy Young, the hard-throwing righthander is, of course, baseball's all-time winningest pitcher with those 511 victories being rolled up over 22 seasons from 1890 to 1911.

Another highly unusual gift came to the Hall of Fame shortly after Johnny Mize was elected to baseball's shrine in 1981. The gift consisted of a large bucketful of red clay soil from the school playground in Demorest, Georgia, where Mize first began playing on the diamond. The contributor was Demorest's school superintendent.

In a 15-year major league career (1936–53, with three years out for military service in World War II), Johnny Mize slammed out 359 homers and averaged .312, while playing successively for the St. Louis Cards, New York Giants and New York Yankees.

Nelson Fox isn't a Hall of Famer yet, but many baseball experts feel he should eventually gain election to baseball's shrine. During a 19-year big league career (1947–65), mostly with the Chicago White Sox, Fox batted a potent .288, lined out 2,663 base hits, and scintillated as a smooth fielding second baseman. After his premature death in 1975, members of Fox's family contributed a batch of the infielder's mementos to the Hall of Fame Museum. These included an unopened pouch of "Nelson Fox's Favorite Chewing Tobacco." Fox was such an inveterate chewer that one of the major tobacco companies produced and marketed his own special brand of chaw.

DRYSDALE ALMOST FAILED TO MAKE IT
TO HIS HALL OF FAME INDUCTION

In the Hall of Fame's first half-century of existence just over 200 players, managers, umpires and executives have been voted into baseball's shrine. A player must wait at least five years after his retirement from the game before he is eligible to be voted upon, and sometimes, unfortunately, a diamond star is elected to the Hall of Fame long after he's gone to the Great Beyond.

In the case of Don Drysdale, the righthanded power pitcher of the old Dodgers from Brooklyn had to endure a waiting period of 15 years before he was elected to the Hall of Fame in 1984. Happily enough, he was very much alive and well when he finally received the call, but he almost missed out.

"Big D," as he was popularly known, posted a 209-166 won-lost record with the Brooklyn-Los Angeles Dodgers over a 14-year period (1956–69), and achieved one of baseball's truly noteworthy records in 1968 when he racked up six straight shutouts while hurling 58 consecutive scoreless innings.

"Election into Baseball's Hall of Fame is the highest tribute an athlete can ever receive." That is not just the opinion of Edward W. Stack, Hall of Fame President, but of thousands of fans as well.

Hall of Fame Induction Ceremonies are always elaborately staged gigantic media events with the newly minted enshrined being called upon to make speeches after receiving the bronze plaques

"Let me go. PLEASE let me go."

recording their deeds on the diamond. Thousands of fans from across the country. always jam their way into tiny Cooperstown, N.Y., when those Induction Ceremonies are held on midsummer Sunday afternoons.

Naturally enough, Don Drysdale, now a radio and television broadcaster with the Chicago White Sox, put together a carefully written speech to make at his induction. When his Chicago White Sox employers heard that "Big D" was planning to take the Sunday off, however, they were irked and told him straight out that his job status would be seriously jeopardized if he didn't show up for work in the broadcast booth that day as scheduled.

"It was touch and go for a while," said Drysdale. But after

Drysdale made an emotional plea to his bosses pointing out that this was a one-in-a-lifetime thing (which, of course, they knew), and after a good bit more wrangling back and forth, he was finally given reluctant permission to travel to Cooperstown for his big day! Strange?

BABE RUTH'S "CALLED SHOT" IN THE 1932 WORLD SERIES

The third game of the 1932 World Series still stands as one of the most dramatic clashes in the long history of the Fall Classic. The October 1 game pitted the Chicago Cubs at Chicago's Wrigley Field against the New York Yankees. New York had already won the first two games of the Series played at Yankee Stadium. Babe Ruth smashed a three-run homer off Cubs starter Charlie Root in the first inning, and in the early going, teammate Lou Gehrig also homered.

In the top of the fifth inning, with the scored tied at 4-4, Ruth faced Root again. With a count of two balls and two strikes, Ruth then seemed to gesture toward the center field bleachers, as if to indicate that's where he planned to deposit Root's next pitch. Or was he merely pointing at Root? Or was he addressing the Cubs bench with an exaggerated gesture, since the Cubs bench jockeys were teasing Ruth unmercifully?

Whatever the message, Ruth delivered on Root's next pitch. He swung viciously and the ball sailed like a rocket toward center field—

then went over the bleacher wall. This titanic blast put the Yankees ahead, 5-4.

Lou Gehrig matched Ruth's two homers by following with a drive into the right field bleachers. The back-to-back fifth ining blasts stood up as the margin of victory as the Yankees, after trading runs with the Cubs in the ninth, prevailed 7-5.

Gehrig, the on-deck hitter at the time, obviously thought that the Babe had indeed called his shot. He said, "What do you think of the nerve of that big lug calling his shot and getting away with it?"

Charlie Root, on the other hand, strongly felt that Ruth never pointed to deep center field before the home run pitch. He said soon after the action was over, "If he had pointed to the home run landing spot, I would have knocked him down with the next pitch."

Babe Ruth himself was content to go along with the called shot scenario, although he never really expounded upon the matter in any great detail.

In 1990, we had the opportunity to interview Billy Herman, who was the Cubs second baseman in the historic game. When we asked about Ruth's "called shot," Herman exclaimed without a moment's hesitation, "I never believed that the Babe called his shot. I was standing at second base, maybe 120 feet away from the batter's box, and though Ruth was gesticulating all over the place, I really don't think that any of his actions indicated that he would blast the ball over the center field bleachers. Still, the legend that the Babe did call the shot grew and grew. We'll never really know what was in Ruth's mind."

There's no question, however, that Game 3 broke the Cubs' spirit as the Yankees went on to win Game 4 by a 13-6 count, giving the Bronx Bombers a Series sweep. Now, more than two generations after that October 1, 1932, clash between the Yankees and Cubs, the legend continues to live on. Ruth's homer off Charlie Root remains unquestionably the greatest moment of his illustrious career and the most storied circuit blast in the entire history of the World Series. Babe Ruth played his final game in the major leagues over six decades ago, but the glory of his achievement continues to live on forever.

MARK McGWIRE, HOME RUN HITTER EXTRAORDINARE

During the 1998 season, Mark McGwire reached his peak as one of the premier home run hitters of all time, surpassing records established by such great sluggers of the past as Babe Ruth, Lou Gehrig, and Roger Maris.

Maris' record of 61 homers in '61 stood for 37 years, until it was first broken by McGwire in 1998, and then by Sammy Sosa, outfielder with the Chicago Cubs, who also breached the Maris standard in the same season. Sosa finished with 66 homers, but McGwire went on to virtually demolish the old mark when he concluded the season with an even 70 circuit clouts.

Even more incredibly, McGwire averaged 60 homers per season from 1996 to 1998—slamming a total of 180 balls out of the park. That is far and away a record. With Oakland in '96, McGwire led the

National League with 52 homers, and then in '97 he hit 34 homers before being traded to the St. Louis Cards on July 31. For St. Louis, "Big Mac" homered 24 more times, giving him a total of 58. And his 70 in '98 gave him 180, or an average of 60 over three incredible seasons.

McGwire also became the first player in history to hit 50 or more homers in three consecutive seasons. Babe Ruth did hit 50 or more homers four times, but never in three seasons in succession.

Ruth's best 3-year total came during the 1926–1928 seasons when he slammed out 47, 60, and 54 homers, respectively for a total of 161. Many baseball historians felt that record would never be broken, but McGwire's three-season total bettered the Ruth mark by 19.

The big difference between the Ruth era and the McGwire era revolves around the fact that homers were not in vogue at the time. The Babe was at his peak, from 1919 until the early 1930s. (During the first six years of his career with the Boston Red Sox, from 1914 to 1919, Ruth was almost primarily a pitcher—in 1919, he began to pitch sparingly, played the outfield almost every day, and hit 29 homers in 130 games.)

Ruth, in fact, on two separate occasions, in 1920 and 1927, personally hit more homers than each of the seven other teams in the American League. In 1920, the "Sultan of Swat" smacked out a record 54 homers and no team in the league matched that total.

In 1927, the Bambino, at the peak of his long ball power, whacked his then record 60 homers, and in that season no single American League team managed to top that total. Philadelphia "threatened" Ruth with 56 four-baggers.

In 1998, McGwire faced competition for the National League home run crown from Chicago's Sammy Sosa. McGwire and Sosa were tied at 66 going into the final weekend of the season. While Sosa was homerless, McGwire hit four in his last two games, giving him 70.

Because there were so few authentic home run hitters in the Ruth era, The Babe really stood out in the long ball department, but McGwire does his belting in a home run crazy period in baseball history.

Baseball's
Funny Moments

Baseball is a zany sport where practical jokes, goofy gags, and loony lines muttered by ballplayers are as much a part of the game as heroic home runs, dazzling no-hitters, and inspiring pep talks. Baseball jokesters range from fabled Hall of Famers and modern superstars to well-traveled reserves and lesser-known bench warmers. Baseball history is crammed full of crazy coaches, oddball owners, and wacky players who have all contributed to the unforgettable mystique of America's favorite and sometimes outrageously funny sport.

HOUSE SITTER

In 1978, the Boston Red Sox, managed by Don Zimmer, met the New York Yankees in a one-game playoff to determine the American League's East Division champion. The game was won by the Yankees on a home run hit by New York shortstop Bucky Dent. In 1983, Don Zimmer was hired as a coach by the New York Yankees, and Bucky Dent was traded from the Yankees to the Texas Rangers. Since Zimmer needed a place to live near New York, he rented Bucky Dent's vacant house in New Jersey. When the Zimmers moved into the Dent's home, they found photographs of Bucky's game-winning home run hit against the Red Sox in 1978 hanging on walls all around the house. The first thing Zimmer did was turn around the photographs of Dent's famous hit—so they all faced the wall!

CATCH PHRASE

Dean Chance was on the mound for the California Angels in a close game against the Minnesota Twins. Chance's battery mate was catcher Hank Foiles. The Angels held a slim lead, but the Twins had the bases loaded. Chance fired a sinking fastball low and outside. Catcher Foiles reached out to catch it, and then jumped up and raced back to the screen to chase down what he figured was a wild pitch.

As Foiles frantically searched for the ball, all three Twins runners scored. The ball seemed to vanish off the face of the earth. It wasn't until the crazy catcher looked into his glove that he realized the ball had never gotten by him. It was wedged in the pocket of his glove the entire time. Foiles only thought he'd missed it!

WORK OF ART

In the 1990s, the St. Louis Cardinals outfield consisted of Del Ennis, Chuck Harmon, and Wally Moon. Ennis, Harmon, and Moon were good players, but they all lacked one vital ability. "The Cardinals have a Venus de Milo outfield," a sportswriter once said. "It's beautiful—but no arms."

GRASS ROOTS

When the Philadelphia Phillies traveled to Houston, Texas, in July of 1966 to play in the Astrodome, some Phillies players were asked their opinions of the revolutionary new artificial turf. Philadelphia third baseman Dick Allen was later quoted as saying, "If cows don't eat it, I ain't playing on it."

SHOE THING

Fresco Thompson, who became vice president of the old Brooklyn Dodgers, was one of baseball's great funny men. His wit was even quicker than his bat. Fresco, who for a while played alongside hilarious Babe Herman in the outfield for the Dodgers, once described Herman's lack of fielding ability this way: "Babe wore a glove for only one reason. It was a league custom." In his later years as a member of the New York Giants, Thompson played for manager Bill Terry and was seldom used. Fresco spent most of his days with the Giants relaxing on the bench in the dugout. One afternoon, he was shocked to hear Bill Terry call for him to go into a game as a pinch runner. Thompson yawned, stretched, and refused to play by saying, "I'd love to Bill, but I just had my shoes shined."

BIRD BRAIN

Joe "Ducky" Medwick was a great player for the St. Louis Cardinals. He also had a wacky sense of humor. During his prime, Medwick visited Vatican City in Rome with a group of famous entertainers. The group was granted an audience with the Pope. Members of the group were introduced to the Pope one by one and announced their occupations. "I'm a singer," said the first member of the group.

"I'm a comic," said the next person to be introduced.

When it was Medwick's turn to meet the Pope, Ducky said, "Your Holiness, I'm a Cardinal."

BULL PENNED

Pitcher Moe Drabowsky, who played for the St. Louis Cardinals during the early 1970s, had a wacky way of passing time, while out in the bullpen. While games were in progress, he often used the bullpen telephone to order a pizza. Once he even called the opposing team's bullpen, disguised his voice, and ordered an opposing pitcher to warm up.

GRIMM HUMOR

Manager Charlie Grimm led the Chicago Cubs to National League pennants in 1932 and 1935, but both of his squads fizzled in World Series play. In 1932, he lost to manager Joe McCarthy's New York

Yankees team 4-0. And in 1935, he was defeated by manager Mickey Cochrane's Detroit Tigers team 4-2. Nevertheless, Grimm had a world championship sense of humor. Once a scout called him up to brag about a young pitcher he'd discovered. "The kid is great," insisted the scout. "He struck out 27 batters in one game. No one even hit a foul ball off of him until the ninth inning."

Grimm paused to reflect on the report and then replied, "Sign the kid who hit the foul ball. We need hitters more than pitchers."

SIZE WISE

Huge Ted Kluszewski played for the California Angels in 1961. Kluszewski, who stood six-feet-two inches tall and had massive, bulging biceps, was given a new room-mate that season by manager Bill Rigney. Big Klu's roomie was Albie Pearson, a great player who stood only five-feet-five inches tall. When Kluszewski first laid eyes on his new roomie, he told Pearson, "I get the bed in our room. You get the dresser drawer." Pearson laughed at Kluszewski's joke. One night later that season, Kluszewski came into his room to find Pearson sound asleep in bed. Big Ted lifted Albie out of the bed without waking him and positioned Pearson's dozing form in an open dresser drawer. And that's where Pearson remained until he woke up.

METAL PLATES

The first baseball game in Berlin, Germany, was played in June of 1912, and the wackiest guy on the field that day was the home-plate umpire. No one knows his name, but they know what he wore to call balls and strikes that day. It was a suit of armor.

LET'S SEE

There is more than one way to get an umpire's goat. Skipper Charlie Grimm didn't always argue with the 20 men in blue to make his point. Once umpire Charlie Moran (who had been a college football coach before his umpiring days) made a bad call against Grimm's Chicago Cubs team. As angry players rushed out to fight with umpire Moran, Grimm got between his players and the ump. Charlie raised his hands to calm down his angry squad and stated, "The first person to lay a finger on this blind old man will be fined fifty bucks!"

SICK HUMOR

Seattle Mariners superslugger Jay Buhner is a fun-loving player with a hot temper and a sick sense of humor. Buhner, who clouted 20 or more home runs per season from 1990 to 1995, can't stomach failure. Once while playing golf with some Seattle teammates, he missed a shot and threw his club in disgust. When that display didn't cool his temper, he tried to toss his entire golf bag but found it tightly fastened to his motorized cart. Since Jay couldn't undo the bag from the cart and throw it, he did the next best thing. He flipped over the entire golf cart.

On the field, Buhner's sick sense of humor can be upsetting to those who witness his most famous prank. Buhner can force himself to vomit at will. Jay calls his sick stunt "blurping" and explains it as a combination of burping and vomiting. Buhner usually "blurps" to nauseate rookie players. However, Buhner once pulled his "blurping" gag in the outfield, which caused fellow Mariners outfielders Ken Griffey and Kevin Mitchell to become sick to their stomachs. In a yucky display of team unity, all three players threw up in the outfield during the game.

TALKING BASEBALL

Pitcher Mark Fidrych of the Detroit Tigers was a colorful character during his playing days. While standing on the mound, Fidrych would talk directly to the baseball he held in his hand. On other occasions, if one of his infielders made a good fielding play, Mark would storm off the mound and offer the appropriate player a vigorous congratulatory handshake before continuing to pitch in the game.

CLOWN PRINCES OF BASEBALL
LARRY "YOGI" BERRA

Hall of Famer Larry "Yogi" Berra, who played for the New York
Yankees and managed the Yankees and the New York Mets, was not
only one of the game's greatest hitting catchers, but also one of baseball's funniest guys. His wacky remarks, side-splitting stories, and nutty
exploits are definitely of funny Hall of Fame caliber:

It's a Repeat

When it comes to understated daffiness, Yogi is in a class by himself.
He once remarked, "It's déjà vu all over again."

A Swinging Guy

Yogi Berra was famous for swinging at and usually hitting pitches out
of the strike zone. However, on one occasion he swung at a terrible
pitch way out of the zone and struck out. "Humph," Berra grumbled
on his way back to the dugout. "How can a pitcher that wild stay in the
league?"

Fan Support

When Yogi Berra visited his hometown of St. Louis in 1947 as a member of the New York Yankees, the fans there staged a celebration in his
honor. After he was presented with numerous gifts and mementoes,

Yogi walked up to a microphone to make a speech. Berra took a deep breath and said, "I want to thank all of you fans for making this night necessary."

Crazy Qualifications

When Yogi Berra was named manager of the New York Yankees in 1964, he was asked what qualified him for the position. Said Yogi, "You observe a lot by watching."

Music Man

In 1964, the New York Yankees managed by Yogi Berra suffered though a difficult losing season. After one really disheartening loss, Berra boarded the team bus and was shocked to hear utility infielder Phil Linz playing happy tunes on his harmonica. Upset by the team's defeat, Berra got into a loud argument with Linz and ended up fining him two hundred dollars for playing the harmonica. The next year when Linz signed his Yankee contract, he got a raise in salary which included a two-hundred-dollar bonus. With the bonus was a letter from Yogi telling Linz to spend the two-hundred dollars on harmonica lessons!

THIS IS WORSE THAN BEING HIT BY A PITCH!

Light Humor

Yogi Berra was playing in a World Series game on an October afternoon when the sinking sun cast a dark shadow across the playing field. Looking out across the diamond, Yogi commented, "Gee, it gets late early out there."

Don't Make Waves

One afternoon in the New York locker room, Yogi Berra was telling some rookie players about his first days with the Yankees. Listening as he worked was Pete Sheeby, the clubhouse man. "I was in the Navy the first time I came in here," Yogi said as he pointed at the clubhouse floor. "In fact, I had on my sailor uniform," Berra added. Then he turned to speak to Sheeby. "I bet you thought I didn't look like much of a ballplayer the first time you saw me, huh Pete?"

Pete Sheeby laughed and answered. "You didn't even look like much of a sailor."

Class Act

Yogi tells a story about his days in school. He said he once took a test and answered every question wrong. The teacher called him up to her desk and said, "Lawrence, I don't believe you know anything."

Lawrence "Yogi" Berra looked at his teacher and replied, "Ma'am, I don't even suspect anything."

JAY HANNA DEAN

Jay Hanna Dean (who sometimes called himself Jerome Herman
Dean) more than lived up to the nutty nickname "Dizzy" given to him
by an Army sergeant while Dean was serving in the Armed Forces.
Dizzy Dean was an All-Star pitcher for the famous St. Louis Cardinals
team known as the "Gas House Gang." The Gang included other zany
baseball stars like John "Pepper" Martin, Leo "The Lip" Durocher,
and Frankie Frisch. When it comes to ranking baseball's all-time wackiest and funniest person, Dizzy Dean's name just might get top billing.

Name Game

In 1934, pitcher Dizzy Dean won 30 games for the St. Louis Cardinals
and lost only 7. Dean figured he was due a hefty raise, so he went to
see General Manager Branch Rickey. "I want a twenty-thousand-dollar
raise," Dizzy said.

Branch Rickey almost fainted. "Judas Priest! You're not worth
that kind of money," Rickey shouted.

Dizzy looked Branch in the eye and replied, "I don't know who
Judas Priest is. My name's Dean and I'm worth every penny of it."

Punny Position

Dizzy Dean was a great pitcher, but he often had trouble retiring New
York Giants slugger Bill Terry. In one game where Dean was matched
against Terry, Bill smashed a liner off Dizzy's leg his first time up. The
next time he was up, Terry cracked a liner that sizzled past Dizzy's

head. On his third trip to the plate, Terry rocked one off Dizzy's glove for a hit. Finally Pepper Martin called time out and walked to the mound from his position at third base. "Hey, Diz," said Pepper, "I don't think you're playing him deep enough."

News Flash

On one occasion, Dizzy Dean was batting when he was hit in the head by a pitched ball. Dean was rushed to a hospital. Baseball fans anxious for medical news about the status of the St. Louis star cheered and laughed when a press report stated that Dean's head was X-rayed and the test revealed nothing!

CHARLES FINLEY

"I don't want to be remembered as a kook," Charlie Finley said, "but as an owner who did his best to make the game better." In a way, Finley got his wish. He is the man mainly responsible for the designated hitter rule which is in use in Major League baseball's American League. However, Finley will also be remembered as one of baseball's wackiest club owners.

Stump the Umps

Boring baseball tasks like re-supplying the home-plate umpire with baseballs were given a hilarious twist in the Athletics' home stadium. Team owner Finley had baseballs delivered to the plate umpire by a mechanical rabbit that popped out of the ground!

The umpires were also given a treat during the fifth inning of every home game thanks to Mr. Finley. Finley had water and cookies delivered to the umps. In fact, the cookies were made by an A's employee named Debbie Fields who later established her own cookie business. Mrs. Fields' baked goods are now very famous.

The Merry Mascots

In the 1960s, Finley was the owner of the Kansas City Athletics. One day, he decided the team might play better if it had a mascot. The mascot Mr. Finley decided on for his Kansas City squad was a mule, whom Finley called "Charlie O.," naming it after himself. He also let

WHAT POSITIONS DO THEY PLAY?

the mule graze in the stadium's outfield.

Charlie came up with another wild animal idea shortly thereafter. Behind the outfield in the Athletics' home stadium was a hill covered with pasture land. Charlie put a sheep out in that pasture and dyed its wool green and gold—the team colors of the Kansas City Athletics.

What a Pitchman

Charles O. Finley had a soft spot in his heart (others said he had a soft spot in his head) for pitchers. In 1965, he signed one of the game's greatest hurlers to pitch for the Athletics. That pitcher was the immortal Satchell Paige. However, Paige was nearly 60 years old at the time, and Finley signed him to pitch just one game.

When Charlie signed pitcher Jim Hunter to a contract, he decided Hunter needed a nickname. Finley loved baseball nicknames. Charlie asked Jim what he liked to do when he wasn't playing baseball. "I like to go fishing for catfish," answered Jim.

"From now on, you'll be Catfish Hunter," Finley announced. To this day, the nickname "Catfish" has stuck with Jim Hunter.

Finley tried to tag a new name on another of his famous hurlers,

Vida Blue, an All-Star pitcher and a Cy Young Award winner. Finley tried talking his young superstar into changing his first name from Vida to "True" so he would be known as "True Blue." Blue absolutely refused, and he kept his first name despite the protests from the wacky Finley.

Clubhouse Rap

The Kansas City Athletics moved west and became the Oakland Athletics in 1968. Charles Finley was never one to stand in the way of progress. He was also an owner who believed in keeping his players entertained. In fact, a batboy for the A's named Stanley Burrell was encouraged to dance in the clubhouse to entertain Charlie's players. That dancing batboy later became rap music mega-star M.C. Hammer.

AH, SKIP IT

Babe Herman's wacky ways are legendary. Babe didn't like to report to spring training, so he seldom signed his yearly contract until the season was about to begin. Everyone thought Babe "held out" each year just to squeeze more money out of the Dodgers team, which might not have been the whole truth. A teammate once asked Babe, "Is it worth skipping spring training every year just to get a few more dollars?"

Wacky Herman, the worst fielder in baseball, replied, "I don't do it for the money. The longer I stay out of training camp, the less chance I have of getting hit by a fly ball."

Bogus Babe

During his heyday, Babe Herman was a well-known celebrity. However, for a short period of time, an imposter made the rounds of New York restaurants and nightclubs claiming to be Babe. "Look," Babe Herman said to the press when asked about the imposter. "Showing up that fake is easy. Just take the guy out and hit him a fly ball. If the bum catches it, you know it ain't the real Babe Herman!"

Smoke Screen

On another occasion, Babe Herman cornered several reporters in the Dodgers' locker room after a game and tried to convince them there was nothing nutty about his behavior. After a long talk, he finished by stating, "I'm just a normal guy." He then pulled a cigar out of his jacket pocket and began to puff on it. Babe didn't have to light the cigar. The stogie was lit the entire time it was in his pocket!

Triple Trouble

HEY, WAIT FOR US!

Could Babe Herman hit! However, he didn't always think straight. One day the daffy outfielder came to the plate with the bases loaded and no outs. He quickly walloped a triple. Unfortunately for Babe and the Dodgers, the triple turned into a double play when Herman raced past two of his Brooklyn teammates on the base paths in his rush to reach third base. The runners he passed were declared out.

JOE GARAGIOLA

Joe Garagiola may not have been one of the game's greatest catchers, but he is one of baseball's best storytellers.

Dough Boy

After his Major League career ended, Joe Garagiola worked as a broadcaster of major league games. He remembers the early days when the hapless New York Mets had difficulty winning games. During that period, he attended a banquet in New York City. When a waiter laid a basket of breadsticks on his table, Garagiola quipped, "I see the Mets' bats have arrived."

Can't Resist

Sports broadcaster Joe Garagiola tells the story of Smead Jolley, a great fastball hitter. Jolley is up at the plate with runners on first and third. The guy on first breaks from the base to steal second. The catcher throws to second. The guy on third sees the throw and starts to run home. The shortstop cuts off the throw to second and fires a perfect strike to the plate. It's going to be a close play at home. At the plate, Jolley watches intently. When the hard throw from the shortstop comes across the plate, Jolley swings and cracks the ball into the out field. "Hey," the home-plate ump yells to Jolley, "What are you doing?"

"Sorry, ump," answers Smead. "I couldn't resist. That's the first fastball I've seen in weeks."

PROTEST MARCH

Earl Weaver recorded 1,480 victories in his 17 seasons as skipper of the Baltimore Orioles. As a manager, Weaver was not afraid to exchange heated words with any home-plate umpire in the league. On one occasion, Weaver got into an argument with umpire Ron Luciano. "I'm playing this game under protest," Weaver screamed.

"Protest? On what grounds?" the ump asked.

"On the grounds of your integrity," the Baltimore skipper shouted.

"You know I have to announce the protest," Umpire Luciano replied. "Are you sure that's how you want me to do it?"

"Damn right" Weaver grumbled. And so the Baltimore Orioles played a Major League baseball game under protest because their manager doubted the home plate umpire's integrity.

MILLER TIME

Having a star player like Babe Ruth on your team can be a mixed blessing, as New York Yankees manager Miller Huggins quickly learned. Ruth, who never paid much attention to training rules or team regulations, made no attempt to hide his off-the-field behavior. Late one night while the Yankees were on the road, Huggins and road secretary Mark Roth were sitting in a hotel lobby when Ruth walked in way after curfew. "I'll have to talk to Ruth tomorrow about the late hours he keeps," Huggins said to Roth.

The next afternoon, the Yankees played a game. In the contest, Ruth clubbed two home runs. That evening Huggins and Roth were again in the hotel lobby when Ruth came strolling in long after curfew.

"He's done it again," Roth said to Huggins. "Are you going to talk to him?"

"I sure am," answered Huggins. As Babe walked by, Huggins yelled out, "Hi, Babe. How are you?"

YOU BURN ME UP

Jamie Quirk, of the Kansas City Royals, pulled the ultimate bathroom joke on pitcher Dan Quisenberry while they were in the bullpen in Boston. When Quisenberry went into a portable toilet in the bullpen, Quirk thought it would be funny to light a fire under Dan. He lit some newspapers and smoked Quisenberry out of the portable bathroom. The crowd roared when Quisenberry rushed out and was caught with his pants down!

FAINT HEART

When Nick Altrock was coaching third for the old Washington Senators, he never missed a chance to take a verbal potshot at an umpire. Once during a game, a Senators batter hit a line shot foul into the stands behind Altrock. An umpire ran over and saw some people in the stands helping a female spectator who was unconscious. "What happened?" the ump asked Nick. "Did that ball hit her?"

"Nah," answered Nick Altrock. "When you yelled foul, she was so shocked that you finally made a correct call, she passed out!"

FUNNY MONEY

In 1970, Bernie Carbo played for the Cincinnati Reds, who were managed by Sparky Anderson. As a skipper, Sparky strictly enforced team rules and regulations. Whenever a player did something wrong,

Anderson was quick to levy a fine. It was also Sparky's habit to donate to charity the money he collected from players in fines. One day, a smiling Carbo came to the Reds' skipper with a question. "My wife keeps asking me why we get so many thank-you notes from the Heart Fund. She can't figure out why I'm making so many contributions. What should I tell her?" Anderson just laughed and walked away.

KINER QUIPS

New York Mets broadcaster Ralph Kiner, who was a great slugger during his playing days, says some of the funniest things. On one occasion, he remarked, "The Mets' Todd Hundley walked intensely his last time up." On another occasion, the ever glib Kiner cracked, "That's the great thing about baseball. You never know exactly what's going on."

KINGS OF DIAMOND DAFFINESS
CHARLES "CASEY" STENGEL

Charles "Casey" Stengel was a daffy outfielder in his playing days, which were spent with the Brooklyn Dodgers, the Philadelphia Phillies, the New York Giants, and other clubs. He also managed the Boston Braves, the Brooklyn Dodgers, the New York Yankees, and the New York Mets. It was Casey's skill as a manager that got him into the Baseball Hall of Fame. He won the World Championship several times at the helm of the New York Yankees. However, Casey is best remembered for his baffling choice of wacky words and his weird way of explaining things that became known as "Stengelese."

The Gag That Bombed

In 1916, young Casey Stengel was a member of the wacky Brooklyn Dodgers squad managed by future Hall of Famer Wilbert Robinson. Robinson, an outstanding catcher with the old Baltimore Orioles, had carved his niche in the baseball record book on June 10, 1892, when he collected seven hits (six singles and a double) in seven times at bat.

Wilbert constantly reminded his collection of diamond clowns of his many personal achievements as a player, especially his exceptional ability to catch towering pop-ups while behind the plate. Robinson wasn't really a braggart; he just wanted to impress upon his young players that he knew what he was talking about when he gave them advice as a manager.

However, jokester Stengel used Robinson's own words as bait for one of baseball's great practical jokes. Stengel, with the aid of his teammates, goaded their manager into making a really wacky wager. He bet Wilbert he couldn't catch a baseball dropped from an airplane circling above the field. With his reputation as a "guy who could catch anything" on the line, Robinson agreed to the bet. He was determined to prove to Casey and his cohorts what a great catcher he was.

The day of the aerial baseball bombing finally came. Ruth Law, one of America's famous female aviators, was hired to pilot a plane with an open cockpit. In the aircraft with her was Casey Stengel.

Standing far below on the Dodgers' training field in Florida was Robinson, wearing his catcher's mitt. Looking on were members of the Dodgers team. When Wilbert was ready to attempt his crazy catch, he signaled the plane above.

Then that sneaky Stengel pulled a shifty switcheroo. Instead of a baseball, he dropped a grapefruit out of the plane. From far below, the grapefruit looked just like a ball.

As the grapefruit plummeted toward the baseball field, Robinson positioned himself directly in its path. The grapefruit slipped through Robinson's outstretched arms, hit him squarely in the chest, and exploded! The force of the impact knocked the Dodgers manager to the ground, where he lay dazed for several seconds. When Robinson regained his senses, his chest was soaked with juice and splattered with squishy sections of grapefruit. Thinking the worst, the future Hall of Famer panicked.

"Help me!" he screamed to the surrounding Dodger players, who were already laughing hysterically. "Help me! I'm dying! The ball split my chest open and I'm bleeding to death!"

When the players continued to howl, Wilbert Robinson smelled a rat, a rat by the name of Stengel. He sat up and, upon quick examination, learned that the only injuries he'd suffered were a bruised ego and a fractured grapefruit. Thanks to kooky Casey Stengel's wacky prank, everyone on the Dodgers squad had a good laugh at their manager's expense. However, Robinson was so infuriated, young Casey had to stay in hiding for several days until the manager forgave Stengel for pulling off one of baseball's funniest gags.

Who's Tired?

Manager Casey Stengel was armed with a quick wit and was always ready to fire off a fast one-liner. On one occasion, the Yankee manager waddled out to the mound to yank a weary pitcher out of the game. "But, Skip," protested the pitcher, who was reluctant to leave, "I'm not tired."

Casey eyed the young hurler and took the baseball from him. "Well, I'm tired of you," Stengel replied as he signaled the bullpen for a relief pitcher.

Bird Brainer

Casey Stengel played some of his best baseball during his years with the old Brooklyn Dodgers. When Stengel was traded to Brooklyn's National League rival, the Pittsburgh Pirates, he knew he'd get booed the first time the Pirates visited the Dodgers. Of course, Casey wasn't the type to take getting booed lying down. When Pittsburgh arrived at Brooklyn's Ebbets Field, Casey cooked up a classic gag guaranteed to please even the rowdy Dodger rooters. When the stadium announcer introduced Casey as a starting outfielder for the Pirates, Stengel hopped out of the dugout. As the Dodger fans began to boo loudly, Casey bowed and tipped his hat. As he raised the cap from his head, a sparrow flew off of his brow and winged its way skyward. The wacky birdbrained stunt quickly won over the hostile crowd. The fans clapped and cheered the return of one of the game's zaniest players … nutty Casey Stengel.

What a Kick!

One day Walter Boom-Boom Beck was having his usual run of bad luck on the mound. Opposing batters blasted pitch after pitch. When the side was finally retired, Beck stormed into the Brooklyn Dodgers' dugout. In a fit of anger, Boom Boom kicked the water cooler. "Hey, calm down! Don't do that," called manager Casey Stengel. Beck smiled, expecting to hear some words of encouragement from Casey. "If you break your leg," Stengel continued, "I won't be able to trade you."

BILL VEECK

Bill Veeck was the P.T. Barnum of Major League baseball. As the owner of the old St. Louis Browns and the president of the Chicago White Sox, Veeck pulled off some of the wildest and funniest stunts in baseball history.

Cool Idea

Bill Veeck had a shower installed in Chicago's center field bleachers in 1977 so fans could cool off on hot days.

Ka-Boom!

The first exploding scoreboard was the brainchild of Bill Veeck. The scoreboard was installed in Chicago, and fireworks exploded every time a White Sox player belted a home run.

Short Game Stopper

The 1951 St. Louis Browns team owned by Bill Veeck and managed by Zack Taylor had some problems. The Browns were in last place in the league and had trouble drawing fans to their games. Showman Veeck decided to spice up the Browns' contests by staging some publicity stunts. One of his all-time best stunts was signing Eddie Gacdel to play for the Browns as a pinch hitter.

Gacdel became famous in the second game of a double-header played between the Browns and the Detroit Tigers at St. Louis in 1951. Eddie Gacdel didn't become a baseball hero for swinging a big bat. He became famous as the smallest man to ever bat in the Major Leagues. Gacdel stood only three-feet-seven inches tall and wore the fraction "1/8" on his back as his number. Since Veeck had listed Gacdel on the official St. Louis roster, the umpire had to let Eddie bat even though the Tigers protested.

Little Eddie Gacdel walked on four straight balls. As the crowd laughed hysterically and cheered loudly, Gacdel trotted down to first base. He was quickly replaced in the game by pinch runner Jim Delsing. The crowd gave Gacdel a loud ovation as he left the field, never to return. Gacdel never batted in another Major League game, but Bill Veeck's little trick on the Tigers was a big success.

VERNON "LEFTY, GOOFY" GOMEZ

Hall of Fame hurler Lefty Goofy Gomez played for the New York Yankees in the 1930s and 1940s. In his 13 seasons as a Yankee, he had only one losing season. As a funny man on the mound, he was never at a loss for producing laughs.

The Naked Truth

One day when the New York Yankees traveled to Boston to play the Red Sox, Lefty Gomez was scheduled to be the starting pitcher in the small, confined Fenway Park. However, when Yankee manager Joe McCarthy went looking for his starter, he couldn't find Gomez in the locker room. After a hasty search of the surrounding area, Joe finally found Lefty. Gomez was crouched in a phone booth, and he was totally naked. "I'm staying in here until game time," explained Lefty. "That way, when I get out on the field, Fenway will look real big to me."

Bright Guy

One dark and dismal afternoon, the New York Yankees took on the Cleveland Indians in a game that pitted Yankee pitcher Lefty Gomez against the Indians' ace fastballer Bob Feller. Feller was one of the hardest throwers to ever hurl a baseball in the Major Leagues. On occasion, some of Feller's pitches went just a bit wild. No batter in his right mind wanted to get "beaned" by one of Bob's blazing bullets. As the skies darkened that gloomy afternoon and the visibility became worse and worse, some of the Yankee hitters started to worry about such a beaning.

Late in the game, Lefty Gomez stepped up to the plate. The field was now covered in shadows. As Feller started to wind up, Lefty lowered his bat, took out a match, and lit it. Gomez held up the burning match to the astonishment of the home-plate umpire. "What are you doing Gomez?" barked the ump. "Can't you see Feller is getting ready to pitch?"

"I can see Feller fine," Lefty replied. "I just want to make sure he can see me!"

Pay Day

Lefty Gomez had lots of funny stories about the days he spent pitching in the Minor Leagues. One of his zany tales was about money problems. Lefty was staying in a boarding house and, due to lack of funds, got way behind in his rent. When the landlady demanded payment, Goofy Gomez tried to talk his way out of the jam. "Just think," Lefty said to the landlady. "Someday you'll be able to say Lefty Gomez the great pitcher once lived here."

The landlady wasn't impressed. According to Lefty's account, she answered, "I know … and if you don't pay me, I'll be able to say it tomorrow."

Full, Thanks

After Lefty Gomez pitched himself into trouble by loading the bases, New York manager Joe McCarthy called time and walked out to the mound. "I just want you to know the bases are full," said Joe.

"Did you think I thought those guys were extra infielders?" Gomez replied.

IT'S ALL IN HOW YOU INTERPRET THINGS

In the spring of 1994, there was a great deal of talk about a rather unusual situation facing the Los Angeles Dodgers. They had a rookie pitcher named Chan Ho Park, who was from Korea. Since he spoke no English, the big question was whether the pitching coach would be able to communicate with him while making a mound visit during a game. Since baseball officials had ruled Park's interpreter couldn't go along for the conference on the hill, this was a very real concern.

Upon hearing all of the fuss, infielder Graig Nettles, always noted for his humor, came up with a great quip. "I don't know what all this concern about the interpreter is all about," he opined. "George Scott (former Red Sox player) played 15 years and he never had an interpreter." Scott, hardly known for his oratory skills or his dazzling articulation, probably was the only one who didn't enjoy Nettles' wit.

MR. REPLACEMENT

Alan Cockrell was a 32-year-old player who had kicked around in many teams' minor league systems as the 1995 season began. In fact, he had logged 1,199 pro games, of which none took place at the Major League level.

The Colorado Rockies were in need of replacement players to start the season. When Cockrell learned he was being considered by Colorado, he was asked if he felt he could handle the situation. He summed up his situation by saying, "When you look at the replacement guys, I not only fit the mold, I am mold."

THE WRY "RAJAH"

Roger Hornsby was one of the greatest hitters ever to don big-league flannels. His career batting average of .358 ranks behind only the .367 lifetime mark of Ty Cobb. Hornsby attributed much of his success to his single-minded devotion to baseball—they say he wouldn't even attend a motion picture for fear it would somehow hurt his batting eye.

He offered an opinion on why baseball is a better sport than golf by saying, "When I hit a ball, I want someone else to go chase it."

TALES OF LEATHER

Two classic stories stand out when it comes to tales of defensive play.

First, a look at Dick Stuart, a notoriously poor-fielding first baseman. The man nicknamed "Dr. Strangeglove" was a Pirate fan favorite despite his shortcomings with the leather. One day, a bat slipped out of the hands of an opposing batter. The bat whirled through the air towards first base, hit the turf, and then bounced all the way to Stuart. The first sacker came up with the bat cleanly, thus drawing good-natured cheers from a somewhat sarcastic crowd.

When asked if that was the most applause he'd ever heard, he responded, "No, one night 30,000 fans gave me a standing ovation when I caught a hot-dog wrapper on the fly."

Likewise, Johnny Mize could hit a ton, but was a leather liability at first base. When Mize was playing with the Giants for manager Leo Durocher, he also became the target of sarcasm. A fan mailed a letter to Leo The Lip which read: "Before each game an announcement is made that anyone interfering with or touching a batted ball will be ejected from the park. Please advise Mr. Mize that this doesn't apply to him."

A'S INSULTS

Two players from the Oakland Athletics came up with scathing insults. First, relief specialist Darold Knowles summed up Reggie Jackson's personality quite succinctly by saying, "There isn't enough mustard in the world to cover him." The flamboyant Jackson was the personifica-tion of being a baseball "hot dog" according to detractors and team-mates as well.

During the glory days of the Athletics in the 1970s, the team owner was Charlie Finley, a controversial figure. Even though the A's won the World Series for an amazing three consecutive years (1972–1974), Finley was not exactly loved by many of his players. One such player was pitcher Steve McCatty. When McCatty learned Finley had undergone heart surgery, McCatty took this stab at his boss, "I heard it took eight hours for the operation … seven and a half to find the heart."

Nettles on Steinbrenner

Like Finley, New York Yankees owner George Steinbrenner is con-stantly making headlines and enemies. Over the years, more than a few of his players have said they detest Steinbrenner because of his volatility and insensitivity. Some of those players went on to change their minds. Others simply changed their teams, at times being traded due to their public comments concerning their boss.

It should be noted, though, that Steinbrenner, a very wealthy man, is also capable of being quite generous. He must have felt gen-erosity (or a forgiving sense of humor) towards Nettles because he put up with a lot from the veteran Yankee infielder. For example, Nettles once said of his owner, "It's a good thing Babe Ruth still isn't here. If he was, George would have him hit seventh and say he's overweight."

The outspoken Nettles is most remembered for his view of the chaotic atmosphere playing for Steinbrenner's Yankees. "When I was a little boy," he said, "I wanted to be a baseball player and join the circus. With the Yankees, I've accomplished both."

MORE SADISM

During a 1995 baseball game, Philadelphia Phillies relief pitcher Norm Charlton was on the mound. He wasn't in the contest long before he let loose with a pitch to San Diego Padres' Steve Finley that was hit back to him a whole lot faster than it had been pitched.

The liner off Finley's bat smacked Charlton directly on his forehead, shocking everyone in attendance. Observers noted they couldn't ever recall so much blood gushing from an injury. Such a blow had ended players' careers in past cases. Remarkably, Charlton was relatively unscathed.

In fact, he was back at the ballpark the next day joking with the media. "I've had worse headaches than this," said the lefty, who broke into the majors with Cincinnati, where he became part of a wild crew of bullpen inhabitants nicknamed "The Nasty Boys." When reporters pointed out that his bruised appearance was quite a sight, he responded, "I guess I'll have to cancel that GQ cover.

Charlton even insisted he came to the park because he felt he was capable of pitching even with injuries less than 24 hours old. With that thought in mind, reporters approached the Phillies manager Jim Fregosi. "Would you actually use him tonight?" they queried. Fregosi showed his ability to employ gallows humor by saying, "Why not? He didn't throw that many pitches last night."

KEN GRIFFEY, JR. SIGNS FOOTBALL UNDER THE MOST UNUSUAL CIRCUMSTANCES

Baseball fans often go to unusual lengths to obtain a free autograph from a diamond star, with one of the strangest attempts coming during a Sunday, August 30, 1998 game between the New York Yankees and the Seattle Mariners before a packed house of more than 50,000 screaming fans at Yankee Stadium.

In the bottom of the fifth inning, a fan wearing a No. 24 Ken Griffey, Jr. jersey bolted from the grandstand along the left field line foul directly at the Mariners center fielder. Almost immediately, security guards descended upon the interloper from all sides. Griffey stood in place, hands on hips, stunned, unsure of what to expect. "You never know," he said later.

The fan proceeded to hand Griffey a regulation-size football and a pen and asked for an autograph, just before being tackled and heaved to the ground. As the security detail gained control of the fan, Griffey inscribed his signature on the football.

As the fan was hauled away to custody, he stretched out one free hand and Griffey handed him the ball. Alas, the souvenir was later taken away by the tightly disciplined Yankees security contingent.

Griffey Jr. has always been regarded as "fan friendly." John Sterling and Michael Kay, who were doing the radio broadcast for the

Yankees, guffawed throughout the curious incident.

Incidentally, the Mariners thrashed the Yankees 13-3 in that game. And the hitting star for Seattle? Why, none other than Ken Griffey, who smacked two homers and drove in five runs!

ZANY UMPIRING IN THE JAPANESE LEAGUES

Umpiring practices in Japan are somewhat different compared to the umpiring ways in the U.S. professional leagues. For example, in a 1973 game played at Tokyo's sprawling Korakuen Stadium, a player began punching an umpire as the result of a disputed call. Several teammates joined in on the pummeling. Then the team's manager came storming out of the dugout. What did he do? Stop the fight? Heck, no. He also began punching the beleaguered ump!

Unlike American umpires, their Japanese league counterparts change their decisions—sometimes two or three times, depending upon the arguments put forward by the players, coaches, and managers. At a June 1974 game between the Tokyo Giants and the Hanshin Tigers at Korakuen, we witnessed a 45-minute game delay because of umpire indecision. All the while, the Japanese fans remained in their seats, quite complacent.

In 1974, Joe Lutz, a former major league player and a Cleveland Indians coach, became the first American to manage a team in Japan when he was appointed pilot of the Hiroshima Toya Carp of the Central League. Lutz resigned before the season was over. Why? Because of a controversial call at home plate that went against his team. On that one call, the umpire changed his mind three times.

MARK McGWIRE'S SYNTHETICALLY MARKED HOME RUN BALLS

During the 1998 home run race between St. Louis Cardinals' Mark McGwire and Chicago Cubs' Sammy Sosa, fans became obsessed with catching the home-run baseballs hit into the grandstands by that duo (especially by McGwire, who outpaced Sosa in the homer derby for most of the time).

From a historical perspective, Sal Durante, a New York fan, became a minor celebrity after he retrieved Roger Maris' 61st home run ball in the right field bleachers at Yankee Stadium on October 2, 1961. Durante reportedly sold the historic baseball for $5,000.

National League officials were cognizant of the fact that any record-breaking McGwire homer baseball would undoubtedly be worth a lot of money on the open market. As the St. Louis slugger passed the 50-homer mark, every ball pitched to him was marked with synthetic DNA to make it identifiable. Thus, there would be no chance for anyone to pass off a "fake" McGwire home run ball.

On the last day of the 1998 season, on Sunday, September 27, at Busch Stadium in St. Louis, McGwire, in his final time at bat, lined his 70th home run into a deep left field luxury-box suite.

After a ferocious scramble, Philip Ozersky, a 26-year-old technician at the St. Louis University School of Medicine, came up with the ball.

Within two weeks, after gaining possession of the ball, he received some 400 inquires from dealers and collectors. Three St. Louis collectors got together and offered Ozersky a cool $1 million. Ozersky hired a lawyer to help him sort through all the offers.

The baseball is considered to be worth far more than $1 million, and now ranks as the single most valuable bit of baseball memorabilia.

One of the wackiest offers for the ball came from a man who identified himself as a distributor for a major American doll maker. Ozersky's lawyer commented, "This guy thinks he can get a million threads out of the ball, and insert one tiny thread into a million dolls. And sell them as Mark McGwire dolls with a piece of the ball in each one. That's not all. Then he wants to put the ball back together with other thread and sell it!"

THE NEW YORK YANKEES— TIGHT WITH A BUCK

The New York Yankees, baseball's most successful franchise, had the reputation of being extremely "tight with a buck"—at least until George Steinbrenner bought the team in 1973.

Take the tale of Babe Ruth, whose relations with the Yankees were strained after he retired from active play in 1935. At the beginning of the 1939 season, he wrote to the Yankees offices and requested a pair of complimentary tickets for opening day at Yankee Stadium. Ruth was curtly told via return mail that he must include his check with his request. Naturally, Ruth, who felt he was grievously insulted, was not present for opening day ceremonies.

Then we have the case of Phil Rizzuto, who often recounted this story when he was doing play-by-play for the Yankees on radio and TV. He recalled the time he hit his first homer for New York at Yankee Stadium early in 1941, his rookie season. As Rizzuto rounded third base, a fan ran onto the field, grabbed Phil's cap off the top of his head, and ran into the stands with it.

The next day Rizzuto received a note form George Weiss, Yankees general manager, saying that $5 would be deducted from his pay for losing the cap. Rizzuto said, "I couldn't help it. That fan came after me like a madman."

Weiss said firmly, "You've got to hold onto your stuff better." The $5 charge stood.

HENRY AARON—AUTOGRAPHS, YES. REGISTRATION SIGNATURES, NO.

When anyone registers at a hotel or motel just about anywhere in the world, he must sign the registration book. But not Henry "Home" Aaron, the great home run slugger.

When Aaron appeared as an autograph guest at a show featuring all living major leaguers who had rapped out at least 3000 base hits, an event staged at Atlantic City's Showboat Hotel and Casino in the fall of 1995, he flat out refused to sign the registry. "No way I'm going to sign that book!" Henry told the hotel clerk.

It seemed that Aaron's fee per autograph at the Showboat ranged from about $50 to more than $100, depending upon the nature of the item to be signed. (Autographed bats are the most expensive.) Aaron simply wasn't going to sign anything for free.

The matter was settled when Aaron's agent signed the registry for him.

IT'S ALEXANDER CARTWRIGHT, NOT ABNER DOUBLEDAY, WHO INVENTED BASEBALL!

John Sterling and Michael Kay have been partners on Yankees radio broadcasts for a decade. Although we appreciate their general knowledge of the game and its wide array of intricacies, they have their zany moments on the radio.

Kay once went into a soliloquy on the beauty and symmetry of the game during a Yankees broadcast early in the 1998 season. Toward the midpoint of the game, a player hit a grounder to deep short, with the shortstop coming up with the ball and throwing in time to the first baseman to get the out. Kay in effect said, "That's beautiful … in the great majority of the cases, if an infielder handles the ball cleanly, his throw to first will get the batter out. The space between the bases, 90 feet apart, is just perfect. Thank you, General Doubleday, for inventing this great game."

The only problem with Kay's analysis is that General Abner Doubleday did not invent the game at Cooperstown, New York, in 1839, where the first ballgame was supposed to have been played. It has been proven that Doubleday (1819–1893) never set foot in Cooperstown and had nothing to do with the development of baseball. Even historians at the Hall of Fame in Cooperstown agree, although Doubleday's mistaken connection with the diamond game is legendary.

Credit for the development of modern baseball, as we know the game, must go to Alexander Joy Cartwright (1820–1892) who organized the first baseball team, the Knickerbocker Ball Club of New York City, in 1845. Cartwright's Knickerbockers played the first organized game on June 19, 1846, at the Elysian Fields, Hoboken, New Jersey, against a club called the New Yorks.

It was Cartwright, an engineer and New York city volunteer fireman, who set the basic rules of the game that stand today, including ending the practice of putting a man out by hitting him with a thrown ball. He introduced the nine-man team with an unalterable batting order, a nine-inning game, three outs per side, and a 90-foot baseline. He also dressed his team, made up of local firefighters, in the game's first uniforms. Most New York teams of that era came out of various firehouses. Barry Halper, the indefatigable New Jersey memorabilia collector, has a wide array of Cartwright materials, including his fireman's hat and horn!

For his contributions to baseball, Cartwright was inducted into the Hall of Fame in 1938. Though there is a Doubleday exhibit in the Hall of Fame, Abner Doubleday was never elected into baseball's shrine.

The next time Kay muses about the wonder of the 90-foot baselines, he should say instead, "Thank you, Mr. Cartwright."

You're the Manager

Baseball fans love to second-guess managers while they are watching a game. After all, part of the charm of the game is deciding what you would do if you were the manager.

Some fickle fans offer their opinions only after a negative outcome. For example, it isn't unusual to hear a spectator bellow, "I never would've stuck with that reliever," after the pitcher has just given up a home run. That second-guess scenario is all too familiar.

On the other hand, some knowledgeable fans will go out on a limb and declare their managerial intentions before a situation has run its course. This chapter affords you the opportunity to be a big league manager and make decisions based on real-life situations.

Read all the pertinent details about a given situation, then make your move. Next, read on to learn what really happened—or what most big league managers would've done in a certain situation.

Of course, the real-life job of managing entails more than just making calls. Consider the plight of Phil Cavarretta, manager of the Chicago Cubs for the 1954 season. As the team entered spring training, Cubs owner Phil Wrigley asked Cavarretta what the outlook was for the Cubs that year. Cavarretta made a serious mistake when he answered his boss honestly, reporting that things didn't look too bright.

Wrigley, who wanted optimism from his field generals, gave him the proverbial ax. Cavarretta became the first manager ever to be fired during spring training. Still want to be a big league manager? If so, read on and begin making your decisions.

TOUGH CALL

Let's begin with a very difficult call, one that confronted San Diego Padres manager Preston Gomez back on July 21, 1970. His pitcher, Clay Kirby, was methodically mowing down the New York Mets. Through eight innings, the Mets had not chalked up a hit.

Now comes the dilemma. Despite the no-hitter, Kirby was losing, 1-0. In the bottom of the eighth, the host Padres came to bat, and, with two men out, Kirby was due to hit. What did Gomez do? Did he pinch hit for Kirby in an effort to rev up some offense, or did he let Kirby remain in the game so the 22-year-old second year pitcher could try to secure his no-hitter?

What Happened

Gomez made a gutsy move that was criticized a great deal—he lifted Kirby for a pinch hitter. What really gave second guessers ammunition for their anger was the fact that the move made no difference. The Padres went on to drop the game 3-0, and the bullpen went on to lose the no-hit bid. Through 1998, the Padres were one of just three teams (not counting 1998 expansion clubs) that had never recorded a no-hitter. (The others were the Mets and Rockies.)

Change of Scenario

If you voted emotionally to let Kirby try for the no-hitter and felt the choice was easy, you aren't alone—tons of fans feel this way. Now, however, let's change the scenario a bit. Would you remain as liberal if the game had entered the bottom of the ninth and was scoreless? Are you still sticking with him? Let's further assume Kirby is tiring a bit, and his pitch count is rapidly climbing.

Finally, for stubborn fans clinging to the thought of staying with Kirby, would it change your mind if you had a hot pinch hitter salivating, anxious to come off the bench? This time, there's no right or wrong answer—it's your call.

Similar Scenario

In 1974, the Houston Astros manager faced a situation much like the Clay Kirby near no-hitter. Don Wilson had worked his way through eightinnings of no-hit ball and was due up to bat in the fifth inning. The manager lifted Wilson for a pinch hitter. Moments later, the new pitcher, Mike Cosgrove, began the ninth by issuing a leadoff single to Cincinnati's Tony Perez for the only hit they'd get that day. The Reds also wound up winning the game, 2-1. The punch line here is that the Astros manager was none other than Preston Gomez.

Perhaps there's no connection, but Gomez managed Houston again in 1975 for part of the season (127 games), then went nearly five years before being hired again as a big league manager. After 90 games as the Cubs' manager, he never had a job as a major league skipper again.

WAS VIDA FEELING BLUE

Oakland A's manager Alvin Dark had a dilemma similar to Gomez's. On the final day of the 1975 season, Dark sent his ace, Vida Blue (with his 21 wins), to the mound. The A's had already clinched the Western Division, so Dark decided to have Blue pitch just 5 innings, then rest him for the upcoming playoffs.

At the end of those five innings, Blue had a no-hitter going. Dark didn't change his mind, though. He went to the bullpen for Glenn Abbott, who worked a hitless sixth inning. In the seventh, Dark brought in Paul Lindblad before turning the chores over to his closer, Rollie Fingers, to wrap it up. The quartet of pitchers managed to throw a highly unusual no-hitter with Blue getting the win. This game marked the first no-hitter by four men.

INTENTIONAL WALK LUNACY

Intentional walks are a big part of a manager's strategic repertoire. Frequently, with first base unoccupied, a team will deliberately walk a dangerous hitter and take its chances that the next batter will hit the ball on the ground. If he does and the defense turns a double play, a volatile situation is defused, and the team is out of a dangerous inning.

Would a situation ever call for intentionally walking a man with the bases loaded? As is the case with many of the plays that follow, this call is based on opinion. However, 99.99 percent of all the managers who ever filled out a lineup card would feel such a move was positive proof of temporary insanity. Believe it or not, such a move has taken place in a big league game, and on more than one occasion!

Two Intentional Incidents

A recent occasion took place on May 28, 1998, when the San Francisco Giants faced the Arizona Diamondbacks. The score was 8-6 in the bottom of the ninth. With two outs and the bases loaded, Arizona manager Buck Showalter ordered an intentional walk to the always-dangerous Barry Bonds.

After Bonds had moseyed down to first, the Giants were within one run. However, the next batter, Brent Mayne, made Showalter look good by lining out to right fielder Brent Brede on a payoff pitch, ending the contest.

The Second Bold Intentional Walk

Showalter wasn't the only manager who made a brazen strategic move in 1998. On May 24 in the 14th inning of a chaotic game, San Francisco manager Dusty Baker definitely went against accepted baseball wisdom. In the top of the 14th, with the game still tied, Giants pitcher Jim Poole handled St. Louis hitters Ron Gant and Delino DeShields with no problem. Mark McGwire stepped up to the plate, and that's when it happened. Baker ordered an intentional walk to the hot-hitting McGwire.

Baker was deliberately allowing the potential game-winning run to reach base. Traditionalists were apoplectic, but Baker had his reasons for the walk. First of all, anybody who followed the game in 1998 knew McGwire was one bad dude. In fact, he had already homered in the 12th inning. That gave him a major league-leading 24 blasts. With a full week to go in May, he was tied for the record for the most homers ever hit by the end of that month. (Later, he did break that record.)

In addition, Baker was following the baseball adage that you just don't let certain superstars beat you—you take the bat out of their hands. On that day, Baker took McGwire's bat away three times with intentional walks.

When Ray Lankford followed with a single, things appeared to be shaky. However, Poole managed to strike out Willie McGee to end the inning without further damage. Ultimately, the move worked since the Giants went on to win 9-6 in 17 innings. Poole said of the walk, "Your first instinct is like, 'No!' Then you realize it's him [McGwire], and you say, 'Oh, well, I guess so.' He's going pretty good right now." Clearly that was an understatement.

Veteran pitcher Orel Hershiser captured the spirit of the event. He said, "Walk McGwire with nobody on? That's a legend. Jim Poole and Dusty Baker will be trivia, and McGwire will be the legend."

WHEN NOT PITCHING IS GOOD

Along the same lines as the Ott intentional walk issue, sometimes not pitching to a slugger or a particularly hot hitter is as much a case of good strategy as, say, knowing when to yank a tiring pitcher from the hill.

In 1969, when San Francisco first baseman Willie McCovey was wielding a lethal bat, opposing managers avoided him as if he were a coiled, angry python. Not only did "Stretch" go on to win the National League's Most Valuable Player award (45 HR, 126 RBI, and a lofty .656 slugging percentage), he was awarded first base intentionally a record 45 times as well. That works out to about three intentional walks every 10 games.

Foxx Hunt

Consider, too, what American League managers did to Jimmie Foxx. During his 20-year career, spent almost entirely in the "Junior Circuit," Foxx amassed 534 homers, enough even now to rank in the all-time top ten. Knowing how powerful "Double X" was, managers often had their pitchers work around him.

On June 16, 1938, Foxx, by then with the Boston Red Sox, was well on his way to an incredibly productive season that included a .349 average, 50 home runs, and 175 runs batted in. On that day, the feared Foxx was issued six walks during a nine-inning game, still good for a major league record. While the walks were not officially listed as intentional walks, it's pretty obvious that pitchers worked him quite carefully. Again, not pitching can be a wise move.

TO PITCH OR NOT TO PITCH, THAT IS THE QUESTION

After all the talk about pitching or not pitching to blistering hot hitters, here's a real-life case. In the best-of-seven National League Championship Series (NLCS) back in 1985, the Los Angeles Dodgers squared off against the St. Louis Cardinals. The winner would head to the World Series.

The NLCS stood at 3 games to 2 in favor of the Cardinals. The Dodgers had to have a win. They were leading 5-4 as the top of the 9th inning rolled around. Then a critical situation developed. With two men out and runners on second and third, the Redbirds mounted a major threat. Even a single would probably score two, giving St. Louis the lead.

To make matters worse for the jittery Dodgers, the batter was Jack Clark, the Cardinals cleanup hitter, who had already crushed 22 homers and driven in 87 runs that year to go with his .281 batting average in just 126 games.

RUTH'S WORLD SERIES LARCENY

It's the 9th inning of the seventh game of the 1926 World Series. Today's winner will be the new World Champion. The St. Louis Cardinals are leading the New York Yankees by a score of 3-2. You are the Yanks skipper, Miller Huggins, winner of 91 regular-season games.

Despite all that success, you are down to your last out. But all is not lost yet—Babe Ruth is on first base after drawing a walk. The game is still alive. If the "Bambino" could reach second base, he'd be in scoring position. A single could tie it up. Not only that, the batter now in the box is your cleanup hitter, Bob Meusel, and Lou Gehrig is on deck.

Meusel missed part of the season with a broken foot, but he still drove in 81 runs. Gehrig, meanwhile, had 83 extra base hits in 1926, his second full season in the majors. As for Ruth, he had swiped 11 bases during the season and was considered a pretty good base runner in his day.

Final Factors

The St. Louis pitcher was Grover Cleveland Alexander. Although he would come back in 1927 to post a stellar 21-10 record, the 39-year-old Alexander was on the downside of his career. He had recorded a complete-game victory just the day before our classic situation unfolded. Baseball lore states he had celebrated the win by going out on the town that evening… and into the morning. They say he didn't even witness the events prior to being called into the game because he was by then soundly sleeping in the bullpen.

Now, having worked flawlessly for 2 innings prior to the walk to Ruth, the game was on the line. He peered in to get the signal from his catcher, Bob O'Farrell, who had a .976 career fielding percentage.

Armed with all the data, what would you have done if you were in charge? Call for a hit-and-run play? Do nothing and let Meusel swing away? Have Meusel take a strike (not swing at a pitch until Alexander throws a strike)? This last would show whether Alexander was getting wild and/or tired; after all, he had just walked Ruth. Would you have Ruth steal to get into scoring position? Any other ideas?

What Happened

Ruth took his lead. Alexander fired a pitch, and Ruth, who had stolen a base the day before, took off for second. O'Farrell's throw easily beat Babe as St. Louis player-manager Rogers Hornsby applied the tag. The Series was over with the Yankees losing on a daring play that most experts felt was also a very foolish play.

Accounts of the game indicate that Huggins actually had Meusel hitting away and did not have Ruth running. The story goes that Ruth was running on his own, creating a terrible blunder. Few, if any, managers would have had Ruth running —it was way too risky.

The Outcome

The Sox skipper, Ed Barrow, made a good call. Although Ruth grounded out early in the game, he tripled-in two of Boston's three runs. In his final at-bat, he sacrificed. Meanwhile, the man who did hit in the ninth spot was a catcher by the name of Sam Agnew. He went 0-for-2 after hitting .166 on the year.

On the mound, Ruth worked eight innings, got in trouble in the ninth, was relieved, then moved to the outfield as the Sox held on to win, 3-2. Boston also went on win the Series 4 games to 2. By the way, during this game, Ruth's streak of 29⅔ consecutive scoreless innings (a record at the time) came to an end.

Quick Quiz

Do managers normally try to steal home in a situation like this? The runner on third can be anyone you choose. If you'd like, select Ty Cobb, who stole home an all-time record 50 times during his illustrious career. (Who wouldn't like that prospect?)

Now, does it matter if the batter is a lefty or righty as long as you have the fiery Cobb barreling down the line as soon as the pitcher commits to throwing the ball to the plate?

O **ANSWER:** Yes, it matters. Most managers feel they'd definitely prefer a right-handed batter in the box when they attempt a steal of home. Back in the 1940s, Jackie Robinson was known to have done it with a lefty in the batter's box, but he was special.

Incidentally, stealing home was rather common in the Cobb era, a dead-ball era in which you'd scratch for runs any way you could come by them.

Lately, swiping home is a rarity. Wade Boggs, a sure future Hall of Famer, says that nowadays, you just don't see it done. "It's probably a lost art. Mostly it's done now with first and third. The guy on first takes off, then the guy on third takes off."

Nevertheless, when an attempt to steal home does occur, you still don't want a lefty at bat. A left-hander stands in the batter's box to the right of the catcher. Conversely, a right-handed hitter stands on the left side of the catcher.

What's the logic involved here? Kevin Stocker of the Tampa Bay Devil Rays explained, "If you're on the right side of the plate, and you're straight stealing, the catcher can see the runner coming and has no one to go around." In other words, there's nothing obstructing his tag.

Or, as Atlanta Braves manager Bobby Cox, perennial winner of division titles, put it, "You want the batter in the right hander's box to help block out the catcher." A righty obstructs the catcher's view of the runner dashing down the line. The catcher may not realize a play is on until it is too late to do anything about it.

There was once a runner who stole home standing up. This happened because the pitcher threw a pitch that was so wild, the catcher was only able to grab it after lunging out of the line of action. Thus, he couldn't even come close to tagging the runner.

THE PLAYER-PITCHER SWITCH

Let's say that the starting southpaw of the Phillies is in trouble late in a game against the Braves. Atlanta has runners on first and second, one out, and their clean-up hitter, a right-handed batter, at the plate.

The Phillies manager decides to relieve his star lefty with his best bullpen hurler, a righty. But he does not remove his star pitcher from the game. He puts him at first base and moves his first baseman to play third base. The relief pitcher gets the batter to hit a short fly ball to left field for an out. There is no advance. Then the manager returns the fielder from third to first and restores his star to the mound, to pitch to the next batter, who is a left hand hitter.

Can a manager switch pitchers this way?

O **ANSWER:** As long as he stays in the game, a pitcher can return to the mound. The pitcher who replaced him, however, has to have hurled to at least one official batter.

Manager Paul Richards of the White Sox used to be noted for that switch. One day he substituted left-hander Billy Pierce for right-hander Harry Dorish when southpaw-swinging Ted Williams was at the plate. Richards kept Dorish in the game, placing him at third base. When Pierce retired Williams, Dorish returned to the mound, retiring Pierce. The displaced third baseman, however, could not come back into the game.

Sometimes Richards used to keep Pierce, a good-hitting pitcher, in the game, too. Richards would put his pitcher at first base. When the situation was right, he would return his good hitting pitcher to the mound.

THE ELEMENT OF SURPRISE

The Yankees are at bat with a runner on third base.

With a count of two balls and two strikes on the batter, the runner on third tries to steal home. The batter, totally surprised, takes the pitch which the umpire calls a ball. Meanwhile the runner is tagged out.

"Don't s...w...i...n...g."

What's wrong with that play?

O **ANSWER:** The runner never—repeat never—tries to steal home with two strikes on the batter. A hitter, when he has two strikes on him, has to protect the plate. So if the ball is close, he has to swing. If he does, the runner could be hit by either the ball or the bat. In either event, the consequences could be disastrous.

The Yankees were guilty of that mistake a few years ago. Roy Smalley was the runner; Graig Nettles, the batter. Don Zimmer was the third-base coach. With a count of two balls and one strike, Nettles jumped out of the way of a pitch under his chin. Zimmer and Smalley assumed that the pitch was a ball, but the umpire called it a strike. On the next pitch, Zimmer thought that the count was three-one, instead of two-two, and he sent Smalley in.

Realizing the situation, Smalley, while running home, was pleading, "Graig, Graig, please don't swing."

Nettles didn't. But the strategy definitely took the possibility of a hit away from Nettles.

IT COULD HAVE BEEN

How important is it that a pitcher be able to cover first base well? It's ultra-important. It's so important that it might have cost the Yankees the 1985 pennant.

In this case, the Yankee pitcher breaks to his left on a ball hit to the first baseman. The throw is in time. But the pitcher, who had run directly across to the bag, overruns the bag in his haste to beat the runner. The ball then comes loose from his glove and rolls down the right-field line. Two Blue Jays score as the game turns around.

What mistake did the pitcher make?

○ **ANSWER:** The pitcher should have "bellied" into the catch. That is, he should have run to a spot on the foul line midway between home and first and cut to his left, running parallel to and inside the foul line. Then, he could have caught the ball while his right foot could be touching the second-base side of the base. In that way, the pitcher avoids contact with the runner and makes the play the safe way.

Ron Guidry had outduelled Dave Stieb in the first game of the big September series with the pennant at stake, and it looked as though the Bronx Bombers were going to finally overtake the Blue Jays. But this basic play turned the game—and perhaps the season—around.

Don Mattingly, one of the best fielding first basemen in recent memory, made the play going to his right, turned and threw. Mattingly made a high throw, very uncommon for him. Phil Niekro, an accomplished fielder, in running straight towards the bag, got his hands up slowly. Normally he would have made that play. When the ball bounced off the pitcher's glove and trickled into the dugout, it allowed two runs to score.

Those runs decided the game, preventing Niekro from recording his 300pth career victory and stopping the Yankees from creeping to one-half game from the American League lead.

The Yankees went on to lose eight consecutive games and were virtually eliminated from the race.

If he had made that play, he would have won his 300th game, and the Yankees might have won the pennant.

That's how important it is for a pitcher to be able to cover first base!

THE BOUNCE SLIDE

In the top of the tenth inning in a tight game, a runner races home on a single and slides without a play being made on him.

The catcher, receiving the late throw, notices that the umpire does not make a call. He rushes after the runner, who is walking to the dugout, and tags him.

Why, in this case, does the umpire not make a call? Is the runner safe or out?

O **ANSWER:** No call by the umpire indicates that the runner is neither safe nor out. On this play, the runner misses touching home plate, so he isn't safe. But since he wasn't tagged initially, he isn't out, either. When the catcher runs after him and tags him, then the runner is out.

When Gil Hodges was managing the Washington Senators, he was victimized by such a play. One of his players slid "across" the plate without a play being made. When the Oriole

The bounce slide

catcher realized that a call hadn't been made; he tagged the surprised runner out.

Hodges angrily faced the umpire and demanded to know how his runner could be out when a play hadn't been made on him. The umpire informed Hodges that when the Senator runner slid, he bounced over the plate.

EVERYTHING TO GAIN

Imagine that Pete Rose, who is known for his hustle, is on first for the Reds with two out.

The batter hits a long fly ball to right field. Rose breaks on his teammate's contact. Just about everyone in the park thinks that the ball is foul. But a strong wind pulls the ball back into fair territory. The ball lands right inside the foul line as Rose, who never stopped running, scores from first on the play.

What's the moral?

○ **ANSWER:** Run hard on every play, especially if you've got nothing to lose. In this case, it turns out that Rose had everything to gain.

Actually, the Yankees' Steve Kemp was the real-life hero of this script. He scored on a wind-blown fly ball hit by Don Baylor.

Asked why he was running all-out on the play, he said, "There were two outs. I had nothing to lose."

My kind of ballplayer.

EIGHT MEN ON THE FIELD

Marty Barrett of the Red Sox hits very few home runs. Understandably, he was very upset when the Yankees' Ken Griffey Jr. dived into the left-field stands at Yankee Stadium to rob the Boston second-baseman of a long ball blast.

Can an outfielder leave the playing field to make a catch?

O **ANSWER:** Yes, an outfielder, or any other player, can leave the playing field to make a catch. The determining factor is whether the fielder's momentum carries him into the stands while he is making the play. If it does, it is a good catch. If the player establishes a stationary position in the stands before he makes the catch, however, the grab is disallowed.

In the situation described above, Griffey timed his jump perfectly and made a sensational catch while bouncing off a fan who was trying to snatch the ball from him. It was a legitimate catch.

If Griffey had mistimed his jump, landed in the stands early, and then caught Barrett's drive, the hit would have been ruled a home run.

But Griffey played the ball perfectly. Only his landing, back on the playing field, was a little less than smooth. Dave Winfield, playing the part of an Olympic judge, gave Griffey a ten on his dive, but only a five on his landing.

UNAWARE

In a real game, in August 1979, the Reds were leading the host Pirates in the bottom of the fourth inning. But the Pirates had runners on first and third with two out. Pitcher Fred Norman had a three-two count on hitter Omar Moreno. On the pay-off pitch, Lee Lacy at first was off-and-running. Catcher Johnny Bench instinctively threw the ball to shortstop Dave Concepcion, who applied the tag to the sliding Lacy. The umpire called Lacy out.

Lacy, thinking his side was out, then got up and walked towards the first-base line, waiting to be delivered his glove for the field. Lacy was unaware that the pitch to Moreno had been wide and high for ball four. He had been forced to advance on the walk.

When his teammates yelled that fact to him, and that he should return to second, Concepcion was waiting for him at the bag with the ball. The umpire called Lacy out for the second time.

Pirate manager Chuck Tanner argued the call for a long time.

Did his argument prevail?

O **ANSWER:** No. When it didn't, he protested the game. But National League President Chub Feeney overruled it on two grounds: one, there had been no misinterpretation of rules, and two, Lacy should have known what was going on.

THEY WON BUT THEY LOST

In a late-season game in 1979, Yankee first baseman Chris Chambliss was warming up his infielders in between innings when the webbing of his glove broke. While he ran to the dugout to get a new glove, Lou Piniella came out to first to continue the warm-ups. When Chambliss resumed his first-base position, Tiger manager Sparky Anderson came out to the plate umpire and said that once a substitute took the place of a player on the field, he was in the game. When the umpire didn't remove Chambliss from the game, Anderson filed a protest. The Yankees went on to win the game, 3-1.

Did Anderson win the protest?

O **ANSWER:** Yes, he did, but the league office considered it a technicality and elected not to play the game over. Sparky won but he lost.

QUICK EXIT?

On this day Tigers manager Sparky Anderson selects a light-hitting batter as this designated hitter, and he putting him in the no.8 spot in the batting order. But when his time at-bat comes in the second inning, the bases are loaded, and Sparky decides to go for the big inning. He sends up a long-ball hitter, Mickey Tettleton, for his DH.

Can he do this?

O **ANSWER:** No, he can't. The designated hitter named in the starting lineup must come to bat at least one time, unless the opposing club changes pitchers. Rule 6.10 (b).

THE UNKINDEST TOUCH

The Mets have a runner on second base, one out, and Eddie Murray at the plate in a game against the host Phillies. Murray lofts a soft fly ball to left-center field. The runner, thinking that the ball might drop for a base hit, goes halfway to third, but the center fielder makes a good running catch.

His subsequent throw to third base, however, strikes a stone and bounces wildly past the third baseman into the Mets' dugout. The runner from second advances two bases on the play, scoring a run. But he doesn't retouch second before he makes his advance.

The Phillies realize this, so the pitcher, when he puts the ball in play, throws it first to second base and files an appeal with the umpire.

Is the run taken off the scoreboard?

O **ANSWER:** Yes, the runner had to retouch second after the catch. Then, while the ball was dead, he could advance. The award of two bases would have been made from his original base. Rule 7.05 (i).

FORCE OUT?

With one out, the Cardinals have Felix Jose on third base, Todd Zeile on second base, and Ozzie Smith on first base. Pedro Guerrero then hits a ground ball to Met shortstop Dick Schofield, who throws to second baseman Willie Randolph for the start of a double play, but Smith beats the throw. Randolph, however, relays the ball to first baseman Eddie Murray for the out on Guerrero.

Murray notices that Smith has overslid second base, throws to Schofield, who applies the tag to the runner before he can scramble back to the base.

In the meantime, Jose and Zeile have scored on the play. However, the Mets argue that the runs shouldn't count, since the inning ended on a force-out double play.

Are they right?

○ **ANSWER:** No, they are not right. The runs score. It is not a force play. It is a tag play. Rule 7.08 (e) play

TWO TRIPS PER INNING

Scott Erickson, the pitcher for the Twins, is in trouble in the bottom half of the sixth inning. The Brewers have Jim Gantner on third, Paul Molitor on second, and Robin Yount on first with one out. Before Erickson pitches to clean-up hitter Rob Deer, Minnesota manager Tom Kelly comes out to the mound, explaining to his right hander how he wants him to throw to Deer.

Erickson, perhaps thinking too hard, proceeds to walk Deer on four straight pitches. Kelly then comes out to the mound for the second time in the inning, and everyone in the ballpark knows what's going to happen.

What?

O **ANSWER:** A second trip by the manager to the same pitcher in the same inning causes the hurler's automatic removal. Rule 8.06 (a).

ONE TRIP PER BATTER

Suppose in the preceding example, manager Tom Kelly had come out to the mound for the second time just after Erickson had thrown ball three to Deer.

O **ANSWER:** The penalty would be greater. The manager or coach can't make a second trip to the mound while the same hitter is at the plate. Rule 8.06 (a). If the manager does, he is automatically ejected from the game, but the pitcher can remain for the duration of the hitter's at-bat. After the batter either reaches base or makes an out, the pitcher is ejected, too.

THE MANAGER'S CLONE

Let's take the preceding situation one step further. Suppose Kelly has already made his one trip to the mound, but after Deer runs the count to 3-0, Kelly yells some instructions to shortstop Greg Gagne, who runs to the mound to converse with Erickson.

Is there any penalty?

O **ANSWER:** Yes. Gagne's trip to the mound would be considered Minnesota's second conference during the same at-bat, and the same penalties that were imposed when Kelly visited the mound twice during the same hitter's at-bat would apply here. Rule 8.06 (a).

The rule wasn't always applied so rigidly. Casey Stengel frequently used to manage through his infielders, who didn't always relish the role of playing manager.

Once during the 1949 World Series, when Tommy "Wild Man" Byrne had walked the bases loaded against the Brooklyn Dodgers, Casey whistled to second baseman Jerry Coleman. That was his signal that he wanted Coleman to visit the mound. Byrne wasn't too happy to see his teammate, though. "What do you want?" he snapped. "I just wanted to know how you're doing," Coleman said. "Fine. You?" "Fine." "Well, since we're both fine," Byrne said, "I guess we've got business to do." "Yes."

Coleman ran back to his position, Byrne released the pitch, and Gil Hodges hit into an inning-ending double play.

Three years later, in the 1952 World Series, when Yankee starter Vic Raschi was struggling, Stengel whistled to second baseman Billy Martin, who dreaded to visit Raschi, who was a martinet on the mound.

"What do you want?" Raschi greeted him, irritated.

I just wanted to know how you're doing," Martin said. "Well, you're having enough trouble playing your own position. Don't come in here and tell me how to play mine."

Martin, with his tail between his legs, scurried back to his position at second. Later he whined to Stengel, "Don't ever send me to the mound again when Raschi's pitching. He'll punch me in the head."

So Stengel didn't get himself in trouble with the rules— but Martin did.

THE PLAYING MANAGER

Don Kessinger, one of the last playing managers in the major leagues, removes himself from the White Sox lineup in the top half of the eighth inning, then assumes the third-base coaching reins in the bottom half of the inning.

Can he do this?

O ANSWER: Yes. Here is Rule 3.03: A manager under those circumstances may continue to lead his team and may go to the coaching lines via his own directions.

THE FAIR FOUL

Suppose the host Padres, in the bottom of the ninth inning, are tied with the Cubs.

The Padres' shortstop leads off the inning with a single to right. The Cubs look for the bunt, but the hitter slaps a single past the drawn-in infield. The next batter moves the runners up a base with a sacrifice bunt.

The Cubs elect to pitch to the Padres' power hitter. He slaps a soft fly ball down the left-field line. The Cub left fielder thinks that he can catch the ball and hold the runner at third. But the ball bounces off the fingers of the glove, in fair territory, into foul territory for the game-winning hit.

The Cubs argue, however, that since the ball landed in foul territory, the umpire must call it foul.

Is it?

○ **ANSWER:** No, the Cubs are wrong. The determining factor is where the ball was touched. In this case, the ball was touched within the chalk lines, so it's a fair ball. Sometimes a fielder will be in fair territory, but touch and drop the ball while reaching across the chalk line into foul territory. In that instance, the ball is foul. At other times the fielder may be in foul territory, but touch and drop the ball while leaning over the foul line into fair territory. In that instance, the ball is fair.

In 1984 the Yankees encountered that problem in Milwaukee. In a tie game, in the bottom of the ninth, first baseman Mike Felder led off the inning with a single. The Yankee infield, expecting Paul Molitor to bunt, was surprised when the third baseman singled Felder to second. Randy Ready then sacrificed the runners to second and third, respectively.

The Yankees, with lefty Dave Righetti on the mound, elected to pitch to dangerous Cecil Cooper, a left-handed hitter. Cooper hit a Righetti fast ball down the left-field line. The left fielder attempted to make the play, but he deflected the ball, in fair territory, into foul ground, where it bounced. In the meantime, Felder scored the winning run.

Yankee manager Billy Martin argued wildly that the ball was touched in foul territory, so it should be a foul ball. But the umpire disagreed and stuck by his decision.

It's a good thing that he did. The video replay showed that the ball was touched in fair territory.

Fair ball. Fair call.

YOU CAN'T DO THAT

The batter singles sharply to right field with a runner on second base. The team's manager, who happens to be coaching at third, waves the runner home.

But when he sees the right fielder charge the ball and fire on the run, the coach changes his mind. He cannot hold up his hands, however, because the runner is not looking at him at the time. So he reaches out and grabs the runner by the right hand and yanks the runner back to third as the outfielder throws a strike to the catcher.

Can the coach legally do this?

○ **ANSWER:** No, a coach cannot physically aid a runner in any way while the ball is a live ball. If he does, as he did here, the runner is called out. You will see the third-base coach pat a player on the rump after a home run. But that is a dead-ball situation. If the coach had done the same thing during a live-ball situation, the runner would be declared out.

Harold "Peanuts" Lowrey, a third-base coach for the Cubs in the 1970's, did that one day to Bobby Murcer, who was trying to score.

THE HASTY RETREAT

Oakland's center fielder is on second base ready to steal third. He gets a good jump on the Yankee pitcher as the batter flies out to the outfield. Running with his head down, the A's player doesn't see the fly being caught, and is decoyed into sliding by the Yanks' third baseman.

In doing so, he overslides third. The third-base coach, seeing what had happened, helps the runner to his feet; since the fly was caught, and the A's outfielder has to return to second, he goes directly back.

What two things are wrong with this play?

○ **ANSWER:** The two things wrong are 1) the third-base coach cannot physically aid the runner, and 2) the runner must retouch the base he has overslid before returning to second.

That very play occurred in a game between Oakland and New York. The A's Mike Davis overslid third, the Yankees' Graig Nettles applied the decoy, and Clete Boyer, a former Yankee third baseman, was the Oakland third-base coach.

The umpire didn't notice Boyer help Davis to his feet, but he did see that the runner fail to retouch third.

Nettles appealed the play. The umpires upheld the appeal. Davis was called out.

MORE DELAYS

Albert Belle, Baltimore's volatile slugger is at the plate. Let's say he gets irate over a strike call you, the umpire, just made. He starts to jaw with you. After a few moments, you get fed up with the delay and tell Belle to get in the box and quit squawking.

What do you do if Belle refuses to obey your orders ?

O **ANSWER:** In this case, you would order the man on the mound to pitch the ball. As a punishment, you would call that pitch a strike even if it isn't in the strike zone. In addition, if the batter still refuses to step in and face the pitcher, every subsequent pitch is ruled a strike until the recalcitrant batter whiffs.

You're the Umpire

Even fans who constantly boo the men in blue must realize how difficult their job is. To paraphrase a famous quote, umpiring is the only game where you must be perfect on your very first day on the job, then improve during the rest of your career.

This chapter provides you with the vicarious opportunity to become an umpire. You'll be presented with some facts, then you make the call. Good luck—you're probably about to learn that it isn't as easy as it looks.

PICKOFF CHICANERY

Say Ken Griffey, Jr. of the Seattle Mariners pounded a ball into the right field corner. The ball kicked around a bit, and Griffey kept digging around the base paths, sliding into third in a cloud of dust. Let's further imagine he called time-out to brush the dirt from his uniform.

Now the third baseman tosses the ball back to the pitcher, a righty. The pitcher straddles the rubber for a moment, then, seeing Griffey stroll off the bag, throws over. Griffey is doomed—or is he? You're the umpire.

What's the call?

○ **ANSWER:** It is not an out; Griffey can stay at third base. In order for play to resume after a time-out, the pitcher must come in contact with the rubber, not merely straddle it. Thus, time is still out, and the play never happened.

AARON AND HIS 756 HOMERS

Every good fan knows Hank Aaron is the all-time home run king with 755 career blasts. But, here's a situation involving Aaron and home runs that many fans don't recall.

Back on August 18, 1965, in St. Louis, Aaron faced Cards pitcher Curt Simmons. Simmons lobbed a blooper pitch to "Hammerin Hank." The superstar right fielder slashed the ball on top of the pavilion roof at Sportsman's Park for a tape-measure blow. As Aaron stepped into the pitch, he actually wound up making contact with the ball while one foot was entirely out of the batter's box.

Does this matter? Was Aaron permitted to trot around the bags with a home run, was it a "no pitch" call, or was he ruled out?

O **ANSWER:** When a batter makes contact with a pitch while outside the box, he is declared out. Aaron would own 756 homers if it weren't for the sharp eyes of home plate ump Chris Pelekoudas.

GREAT CATCH NULLIFIED

Back in 1982, Terry Harper of the Atlanta Braves made a great catch that, due to an umpire's call, wasn't a catch. On September 26, in the middle of a pennant race, the Braves were playing the San Diego

Padres. In the third inning, San Diego's Gene Richards lofted a ball to left field. Harper speared the ball after making a long run. He caught the ball in fair territory, then crossed into foul territory.

Running as quickly as he was, he needed a good four long strides to slow down. Those strides, though, put him in contact with a low bullpen railing. He grabbed at the railing to brace himself before tumbling into the bullpen area.

At about that time, he dropped the ball. Now the rule states that a ball that is dropped by a player immediately following contact with a wall is a live ball—no catch has been made. That's why umpire Ed Vargo ruled Harper's play a "no catch," and that's why the speedy Richards was able to cruise around the bases with an inside-the-park home run. To this day, Braves fans feel cheated by Vargo's interpretation that Harper hadn't held on to the ball long enough to validate the catch. They believe that the time that passed from the "catch" in fair territory until Harper hit the fence, including his many long steps holding on to the ball, were sufficient to prove it was a catch. Even an NBA official would've called Harper for traveling on this play, but the ump's call stands, as always.

ANOTHER TRICKY OLDIE

The year is 1930, and the pitcher is Burleigh Grimes, a man who later retired with 270 career wins. Grimes goes to his mouth and loads up the baseball with a nasty concoction of chewing tobacco and saliva.

If you were working that game, what would your call be?

○ **ANSWER:** Absolutely nothing. Although the spitball was out-lawed in 1920, there was a grandfather clause that permitted a hand-ful of pitchers to continue to throw their specialty pitch. The last man to legally throw a spitter was none other than Hall of Famer Burleigh "Ol' Stubblebeard" Grimes in 1934.

MONDAY, MONDAY

On May 10, 1977, the Montreal Expos were at home facing the Los Angles Dodgers. Warren Cromartie tattooed a long drive to center field. Rick Monday gave chase. Although he got close to the ball, it struck the wall over his head. Then it ricocheted off the wall, cracked Monday on his forehead, and rebounded over the wall. Is this play basically the same as Canseco's, or does the fact that it first bounced off the wall change things?

What do you award Cromartie?

○ **ANSWER:** Once it hit the wall, it was considered to be a "bounding ball." Such plays result in a ground-rule double, not a home run.

ANOTHER HIT-BY-PITCH SCENARIO

Must a batter make a legitimate effort to avoid getting hit by the ball, or is the fact that he was hit sufficient to earn a free trip to first base?

O **ANSWER:** The batter must try to dodge the pitch. Perhaps the most famous case involving this rule occurred in 1968. Don Drysdale, Los Angeles's standout right-hander, was in the midst of a fantastic streak of shutout innings.

In a game versus the Giants, he faced a bases-loaded, no-outs situation. Dick Dietz, the San Francisco catcher, was at the plate with a 2-and-2 count. Drysdale came in tight with a pitch that hit him. Dietz got ready to stroll to first base, forcing in a run.

But wait a minute—home-plate umpire Harry Wendelstedt ruled that Dietz had made no move to avoid the pitch. Despite an argument that raged on and on, the ruling stood, and the pitch was ball three.

When Dietz proceeded to fly out, Drysdale's shutout streak continued, eventually stretching to 58 2/3 innings. Incidentally, that record was later broken by another Dodger, Orel Hershiser.

THE FAKE OUT

Let's suppose that in the top of the 15th inning, in a game between Minnesota and Chicago, the Twins take a one-run lead.

But in the bottom half of the inning, Chicago's right fielder singles with one out. Then on a long fly ball, he tags up and runs to second. It is obvious to almost everyone in the ball park, including the runner, that he had left first too soon.

The Indian manager comes out to the mound to show the relief pitcher how to properly appeal the play. The pitcher takes his stretch, steps off the rubber, and, instead of throwing to first for the appeal, looks at second. When the runner sees the hurler look at second, he fakes a run to third. The pitcher reacts by faking the runner back to second.

What effect does the fake have on the appeal at first?

O **ANSWER:** The Indian pitcher cannot now make an appeal at first. When he bluffs a throw to second, he forfeits his legal right to make an appeal play at first.

In a real 15-inning contest in the American League, the Brewers tried to come from behind against the Indians.

Charlie Moore, the runner, left too soon on a fly ball. After the ball was returned to the infield, Cleveland manager Jeff Torborg went out to the mound to show pitcher Victor Cruz how to conduct an appeal. When Cruz looked at second, however, he forgot everything he was told. He bluffed a throw to catch Moore at second and thereby lost the right to appeal at first.

No appeal play, no out.

THE RUN STEALER

Sometimes, though a runner misses a base, he can change a negative into a positive.

Let's say one man is at first base, with a runner in front of him at second. That was the scene in a game at Detroit. There are two out. A Tiger batter lines a single to left center. One run scores and the hitter ends up on third. But he missed touching second. Both the Brewers and the Tigers know it.

The Brewers appeal the play. But, as the Brewers pitcher steps off the rubber, the runner dashes for home. The pitcher throws to the catcher just in time to nip the speedy runner.

What mistake did the pitcher make?

O **ANSWER:** The pitcher should have thrown the ball to second. If he had continued his appeal play, the runner would have been out at second, and no run would have scored. As it is, the runner is called out at the plate, the inning is over, but one run counts. Give the runner credit for a heads-up play. He is the reason why one run scores. If he had been safe at home, he would have scored another run.

In an actual game, Ron LeFlore of the Tigers got credit for that identical heads-up play against the Brewers. After he had missed second and was on third, the Brewers, appealing, put the ball in play. As their pitcher turned to throw to second, LeFlore broke for home. The startled pitcher broke his stride toward second, whirled, and fired to his catcher just in time to nip the runner.

LeFlore had nothing to lose. He was already out at second. If he had beaten the throw to home plate, he would have scored a second run for the Tigers.

THE INFIELD FLY

The Tigers, with men on second and first, have no out in the top of the eighth inning. The batter lofts a soft fly ball behind second base. The center fielder of the Brewers comes in; the second baseman goes out. Either one of them can catch the ball easily.

When the umpire sees the second baseman settle under the ball, he calls the batter automatically out on the infield fly rule. But the fielder drops the ball, and other players on the field lose their train of thought. The runner on second, believing the batter is safe on the error, runs to third, thinking that he is forced. The second baseman's throw beats him to the base, but the third baseman commits an error, too. He doesn't tag the runner. Instead, he steps on third for the "force."

Three questions: 1) *Can an umpire call the infield fly rule when the defensive man is in the outfield?* 2) *Who gets charged with errors on the play?* 3) *Is the runner called back from third base?*

O First, the umpire can call the infield fly rule on an outfield play. The rule permits the umpire to make the call any time the infielder can make the play with ordinary effort.

O Second, there were two errors on the play: one of commission (the second baseman's) and one of omission (the third baseman's). However, since the second baseman's error confused the runner into running, he is charged with a miscue by the official scorer.

O Third, the runner on third base is not called back to second. In an infield fly play, the runner can advance at his own risk.

That play occurred in a 1956 game between the Braves and the Pirates. The Braves, with Frank Torre at bat, had Bobby Thomson on second and Bill Bruton on first. Pirate Dick Groat, an MVP winner four years later, dropped the ball and threw it to third baseman Gene Freese in time for the out. But Freese didn't tag Thomson; so the runner at third was safe, and Bruton moved up to second on the play.

There were three errors on the play: Groat's, Thomson's, and Freese's. But only Groat got officially charged with one.

The Pirates won the game, though, 3-1.

Not often is the league president in the stands when something peculiar happens.

THE UMPIRE ALWAYS WINS

The batter takes a pitch that is called a strike. The hitter disagrees with the call. The hurler pitches again and the batter takes again. The umpire calls another strike. By this time, the batter who is furious with the umpire's calls against him, steps out of the batter's box and argues vigorously. The umpire orders him to resume his hitter's position. He refuses.

What does the umpire do?

O **ANSWER:** The umpire orders the pitcher to throw the ball. The arbiter calls an automatic strike for every pitch that is made while the hitter is out of the batter's box. At any time, the hitter can step into the box and resume the count from that point.

Frank Robinson, when with the Reds, got called out on such a play in 1956, his rookie year. He argued about a called second strike in a game against the Giants. Umpire Larry Goetz told him to get back in the box. Robinson refused.

Goetz ordered the Giants' Steve Ridzik to pitch, and called "Strike three" while Robinson was still disputing the previous call!

WHAT'S THE PITCH?

"Get up off second base...you don't own it"

In a hypothetical case, the star hitter of the Red Sox is on third base, with the next batter at the plate.

When the Texas pitcher goes into his windup, the third-base umpire calls, "Balk!" But the hurler pitches the ball anyway and the batter bloops a double to left. The runner on third, who had heard the umpire call a balk, remains on third. The batter who hit the double clutches second. In fact, he refuses to leave the base.

How does the umpire resolve this predicament?

O **ANSWER:** Once again, the balk takes precedence; so the umpire lets the runner from third score and returns the batter to the plate. When the batter refuses to leave second base, the umpire ejects him from the game, and places his substitute at the plate.

In a real-game situation, Lou Piniella of the Yankees, who relished every hit he ever got, refused to leave second under similar circumstances. He had to be kicked out of the game before he would give up his double.

THE CUNNING CATCHER

The Mets' catcher is noted for thinking all the time. The following hypothetical example points it out:

The Braves' clean-up hitter is at bat with a man on first, one out, and a three-two count on him. As the Mets' hurler pitches, the runner breaks for second. The batter checks his swing and the plate umpire calls, "Ball four!" The Braves' first-base coach yells to the runner to stand up. But the catcher throws to second anyway; and the Mets' second baseman makes an easy tag on the runner, who has slowed down.

Then the Mets appeal the swing. The first-base umpire says the batter broke his wrists, which constitutes a swing. Strike three.

Is it a double play?

O **ANSWER:** No, it is not a double play. The runner cannot be penalized for the umpire's mistake. The runner, misled by the false signal, slows down. But there is no guarantee that the runner would have stolen the base had he run hard all the way. The umpire calls the batter out, but puts the runner back on first.

Thurman Munson of the Yankees was such a catcher. In the mid-1970's, he pulled off the identical play. He thought he should have had a double play.

On defense, as an offense, Munson was always thinking one out ahead of the game.

TEAMWORK

The Red Sox have a runner at third base, and one out. The batter hits a long fly ball to right center against the Yankee pitcher. The ball deflects off the right fielder's glove and floats into the center fielder's mitt.

Two questions: 1) *Is the batter out?* and 2) *can the runner tag up after the ball touches the right-fielder's glove?*

○ A fly ball that is deflected off one outfielder's glove into another one's is a legal out. The batter is out.

○ A runner can legally tag up and advance as soon as a fielder touches the ball. He does not have to wait until a fielder "possesses" the ball.

On a play just like this, at Yankee Stadium in the late 1950's, Hank Bauer got the assist and Mickey Mantle, the putout. There was no runner on third. The batter got "put out."

INSIDE THE LINES

Suppose the Red Sox are at bat with runners on second and first with no out in a game against the White Sox.

The batter drops a bunt down the first-base line. The White Sox catcher picks the ball up and throws it to the first baseman. But the batter, who is running inside the first-base line, is hit by the throw. The ball bounds down the right-field line, allowing the runner on second to score. That run turns out to be the deciding one.

Does it count?

○ **ANSWER:** The run shouldn't count, if the umpire sees the play the same way we do. In running the last 45 feet to first base, the batter-runner has to run within the three-foot line that parallels the base line for that distance. If he is hit by the throw when inside or outside that area, he should be called out and the ball declared dead.

This controversial play occurred in the 1969 World Series between the Mets and the Orioles. With runners on first and second, no out, and a tied game in the

"That's my elbow"

bottom of the tenth inning, J. C. Martin, the Mets' batter, dropped a bunt down the first-base line.

Pete Richert, the pitcher for the Orioles, fielded the ball and threw it to first. Martin was running inside the first-base line. The throw hit Martin on the arm and bounced into foul territory while Jerry Grote of the Mets sprinted home with the winning run.

Most observers thought that Martin was clearly out of the base lines and should have been declared out. The umpire saw the play differently, however. His was the vote that counted.

The Mets' run counted, too.

A CATCHY SITUATION

The Reds and Red Sox are tied 1-1 in the bottom half of the ninth inning. In Game 3 of the 1975 World Series, they are also tied at one game apiece.

Cesar Geronimo leads off the Reds' inning with a bloop single. Then the next batter drops down a bunt right in front of the plate. But he is slow to move out of the batter's box. Red Sox catcher Carlton Fisk has to shove the batter out of the way with his glove hand and pick the ball up with his bare hand. Fisk's throw beats Geronimo by plenty of time at second; but because of the bodily contact at the plate, his off-balance throw goes into center field. Geronimo continues to third. The Red Sox want the batter to be called out for interference. In fact, they want two outs, for that's what they would have gotten, if Fisk's throw were on the mark.

What did they get?

○ **ANSWER:** They got nowhere. The plate umpire disallowed the appeal, claiming that the contact was accidental, not purposeful. Joe Morgan, the next batter, singled, Geronimo scored, and the game was over.

That play might have cost the Red Sox the 1975 World Series. The Reds went on to win the World Series in seven games. Had the call gone the other way, the Red Sox might have won Game 3. If they had, they would have won the World Series in six games.

THE TRAP-BALL TRAP

Let's suppose there is a runner at first base with one out; the batter is hitting against the opponents' star pitcher.

The hitter loops a ball to right field, and the outfielder either catches it or traps it. One umpire calls the play a catch; another, a trap. The runner at first, who is confused, finally decides to run to second. One umpire calls him safe; the other umpire, out.

How do the umpires resolve this contradictory situation?

○ **ANSWER:** The umpires are in a tight spot on this one. The only way out is compromise. They allow the runner to stay at second, but call the batter out.

The Mets and the Reds had a similar situation. The Cincinnati outfielder made such a good try that he confused the umpires. He also confused the Met base runner.

The only way out, the umpires concluded, was to give a little and to take a little. Neither the Mets nor the Reds argued too long, since each got something: the Mets, a base; the Reds, an out.

INSTANT REPLAY

Can the instant replay camera cause a pitcher's ejection?

O No, but it certainly created a furor during the 1992 season. Tim Leary, a pitcher for the New York Yankees, got off to a bad start early in the season. Suddenly he righted himself with three consecutive victories toward the middle of June. Then, in defeating the host Orioles one night, he threw an errant pitch that broke Chris Hoiles's wrist. Johnny Oates, Baltimore's manager, was suspicious of the pitch that sidelined Hoiles. While the game continued, he began to collect the discarded balls and place them in a bucket. According to him, they were all defaced. When he had enough evidence, he presented the balls to the homeplate umpire.

The umpire, who didn't have to go out to the mound, did so anyway a few pitches later to search Leary. He found nothing! The diamond-vision camera on the center field scoreboard, however, detected Leary removing a substance—it was thought to be sandpaper—from his glove and putting it in his mouth. The umpire didn't see Leary do it. Oates, who saw it on the screen, asked the umpire to look in Leary's mouth. The umpire, who said it was beyond his authority, refused.

The next day the diamond-vision film excerpt was shown on television stations all over America. There was a demand for action on the part of the league office. President Bobby Brown called Leary in for a meeting, but he let him off with a warning.

Nothing in the rule book says an umpire's or league office's decision can be influenced by the view on an instant replay camera.

After the incident, Leary was no longer effective with the Yankees, though, and in late August he and his huge ERA were shipped to the Mariners.

SHARING AN AT-BAT

Casey Stengel is playing with his batting order and alternating Phil Rizzuto and Billy Martin in the number one and number-eight spots. On Friday, he had Martin batting first and Rizzuto eighth. On Saturday Martin steps into the batter's box to begin the game at Briggs Stadium in Detroit. Tiger pitcher Hal Newhouser runs a count of no balls and two strikes on Martin before Rizzuto realizes he is the named lead-off batter for the

"Casey says it's my turn to bat."

Yankees for this game. The "Scooter" rushes up and takes Martin's place in the batter's box. On Newhouser's next pitch Rizzuto swings and misses.

Is anyone called out for batting out of order here? Who is charged with the strikeout?

○ **ANSWER:** Rizzuto, as the proper batter, gets charged with the strikeout. No one is called out for batting out of order. The proper batter may take his place in the batter's box at any time before the improper batter becomes a runner or is put out, and any balls and strikes shall be counted in the proper batter's time at bat. *Rule 6.07 (a)(1).*

THE QUICK PITCH

Reggie Jackson used to take a lot of time to get ready in the batter's box. In this hypothetical situation, he is still a Yankee, and he is batting with a three-two count with no one on base against a crafty Red Sox hurler.

The Red Sox pitcher fires a strike right down the middle of the plate before Jackson is set, but the umpire calls it a quick pitch.

What's the penalty?

○ **ANSWER:** The umpire calls the pitch a ball. That makes four on Jackson, so he goes to first base. *Rule 8.05 (e).*

Would there have been a ball call if there had been runners on base? No, it would have been a balk. A runner at third would score, a runner at first would go to second, etc. Reggie would remain at the plate with a three-two count. *Rule 8.05 (e).*

It happened in the fourth and final game of the 1928 World Series, Bill Sherdel of the Cardinals "slipped" a third strike by Babe Ruth, but plate umpire Charles Pfirman disallowed the offering, calling it a quick pitch. A ball was added to the Babe's count, and then Ruth hit his third home run of the game (for the second time in World Series play). All of his homers that day were solo shots.

HOW HIGH CAN A PITCH GO?

Is there any height limit to the trajectory of a hurler's pitch?

O **ANSWER:** No, the rule book doesn't cover the subject. Truett "Rip" Sewell of the 1943 Pirates was delighted to find that out. One day during the season, he became the first major league pitcher to throw a lob to the plate. Some viewers said that the pitch rose almost thirty feet above the ground.

Sewell had a number of other pitches that were effective: fastball, curveball, slider, forkball, and change-up. In fact, he posted a league-leading 21 wins that season. But he wanted the hitter to be thinking of his "eephus pitch." It helped to set up some of his other pitches.

"Why can't he pitch it straight"

Sewell frustrated National League hitters for four years with the lob pitch. None of them ever hit it for a home run. One day Eddie Miller of the Reds was so frustrated that he caught the pitch and fired it back to Sewell. The home-plate umpire called that pitch a strike.

There's a climax. It occurred in the 1946 All-Star Game, which the American League won, 12-0. In that game, Ted Williams hit two home runs and drove in five runs in his home stadium, Fenway Park. One of his home runs came against Sewell's "eephus pitch." Williams had thought about the possibility of seeing the pitch before the game. He concluded that the only way anyone could hit the ball out of the park was by running up on it. When he faced Sewell, he guessed right on the pitch, ran up on it, and with his feet in the batter's box timed it perfectly. The ball sailed deep into the right-center field bleachers for a home run—the first and only one that was ever hit off Sewell's "eephus pitch."

How high can a pitch go? Williams proved that it could go very high.

HOW CLOSE CAN "THE BARBER" THROW?

Sal Maglie, pitcher with the New York Giants in the early 1950s, was called "The Barber," for two reasons. One was because he didn't shave on the day of a game, and he had a heavy dark beard. The second was because his pitches "shaved" the heads of opposing hitters, especially those of the Brooklyn Dodgers.

Quite often the Dodger players suspected that Maglie's "purpose pitches" were signaled by Giant (skipper) Leo Durocher, who managed the Dodgers from 1939 to 1948. Dodger fans and players had a love-hate relationship with Durocher.

Let us hypothesize that in 1954 Maglie knocked down slugger Gil Hodges three straight times. Then, with the winning run on second base and two out in the bottom of the ninth inning at Ebbets Field, he threw so close to Hodges' head that he had to fall to the ground.

Would Maglie have been ejected from the game? Would Durocher have been thrown out, also?

O **ANSWER:** Probably not. The plate umpire undoubtedly would have warned the pitcher and turned in a report to the league office, which would have resulted in a fine being levied against him. Durocher may or may not have been fined, also. *Rules 9.01 (d) and 9.05 (a).*

But umpires and head-hunting pitchers got away with much more in those days than they do today. Dizzy Dean of the Cardinals, for example, once knocked down eight consecutive Giant batters in the mid-1930s.

Back in the 1950s, hitters were supposed to retaliate with their own methods. One summer afternoon in 1956, when Maglie was pitching for the Dodgers against the Giants, "The Barber" knocked Willie Mays down on two consecutive pitches. The umpire warned Maglie, who defended himself by saying that "my fingers were sweating and the balls just slipped out."

"Tell Willie I'm sorry," Maglie said to the plate umpire.

Willie hit the next pitch for a long home run. As Mays circled the bases, he delivered his own "knockdown" to Maglie, when he told the third base umpire, "Tell Sal I'm sorry."

BATTER'S INTERFERENCE?

The Cincinnati batter, trying to protect Barry Larkin, who is running from first on the pitch, swings at Phillie's pitcher Terry Mulholland's offering. His big swing misses, but his bat comes all the way around and hits Darren Daulton in the head just after he has released the ball on his throw to second base. Nevertheless, Daulton manages to throw Larkin out.

In another incident Mackay Sasser of the 1992 Mets got a bloody nose when a Pirate batter, Barry Bonds, hit Sasser's nose on his back swing.

Was the batter called out in these cases?

O **ANSWER:** No. If the batter had interfered with the catcher's fielding or throwing by stepping out of the batter's box or making any other movement which hinders or impedes the catcher's play, he is out. Also, he is out if the umpire thinks his act is intentional. However, the batter is not out if any runner who is attempting to advance is thrown out. *Rule 6.06 (c)*

Exception: If Larkin had reached second safely, the batter would have been called out.

In May of 1986, there was an enactment of this play. The Yankees, who were playing the Rangers, had Henry Cotto at the plate and Gary Roenicke at first. Roenicke was running on the pitch, Cotto swung through the pitch and hit catcher Don Slaught, who was attempting to throw the runner out, in the head. Slaught's throw sailed into center field, and Roenicke raced to third on the play.

In this case, Cotto was called out on batter's interference, and Roenicke was returned to first base. The ball became dead as soon as the interference took place. *Rule 6.06 (c)*.

BAT COLOR

Ball players are superstitious about many things, some about their bat. Babe Ruth used a black bat that he called "Black Betsy." It was his special home run stick. George Foster used black bats, too. They helped him to hit 52 home runs in 1977. Bats like the ones he used are known to have a "Foster Finish."

Tan bats that have a light stain are said to have the "Hornsby Finish." They were named after Rogers Hornsby, who used them en route to compiling a .358 lifetime batting average.

Two-tone bats are modeled after the ones that Harry "The Hat"

Walker used. Walker won a batting title in 1947.

These natural shades are allowed.

Are there any shades that are disallowed?

○ **ANSWER:** No colored bat may be used in a professional game unless it has been previously approved by the Rules Committee. *Rule 1.10 (d)*.

There are exceptions to every rule, though. In 1947, Jerome "Dizzy" Dean was broadcasting baseball games for the St. Louis Browns, who were having their typically dismal season—both in the league standings and at the gate. For the Browns' final game of the season at Sportsman's Park, management asked Dean to suit up and pitch three innings. Always happy to provide a lark, Dizzy willingly went along with the gimmick to lure 20,000 or more paying customers to the park.

Six years after Dean had officially retired, he pitched three scoreless and hitless innings. He also went one-for-one at the plate. (During his career, he batted .225 and hit eight home runs.) The color of the bat he used that day was red, white, and blue. Up until the end, the Diz was "colorful."

One additional story of bat shades comes to the author's mind. When he was a teenager, he and his family were listening to a Phillie vs. Pirate's game on the radio. Going into the bottom of the tenth inning, the score was tied 1-1. Suddenly the Philadelphia broadcaster got excited. He gushed, "Uh-oh, Ralph Kiner's coming to the plate, and he's carrying his black bat with him. That's his special bat, his home run bat. That's the one he uses when he wants to end the game."

It was hard to believe that the announcer actually thought the shade of Kiner's bat could dictate the outcome of the game, as though it were some sort of talisman. But two pitches later, Kiner hit a ball over the roof in left field to end the game. It could make one a "true believer" overnight.

DOUBLE PENALTY

An Oakland A's batter is at the plate in the top half of the seventh inning with two out, a three-two count, and the bases loaded. Just as the Mariner pitcher is about to go into his wind-up, the batter steps out of the box and requests the umpire for time-out. The arbiter doesn't give it to him! The pitcher pitches. Scott Bradley, the Seattle catcher, has to jump to prevent the pitch from sailing for a wild pitch.

What happens next?

O **ANSWER:** The pitch, though wild, is called an automatic strike. The batter is out and the inning is over. The umpire doesn't have to give the batter time-out if he feels that it was requested too late or for the wrong reason. It is the batter's responsibility to know whether the time-out has been granted. *Rule 6.02 (b) and (c).*

Jose Canseco of the A's got called out on such a play during the 1992 season.

THE CHECKED SWING

The visiting Braves are playing the Mets at Shea Stadium. Atlanta's John Smoltz is pitching to Vince Coleman, the New York center fielder. With two strikes on him, Coleman checks his swing on a borderline pitch. Plate umpire Gary Darling calls the pitch a ball, but catcher Greg Olson appeals the call.

The plate umpire asks third-base umpire Dana DeMuth for his angle on the swing. DeMuth signals that the batter swung at the pitch. Strikeout. Coleman then engages in a heated argument with DeMuth. Darling, who is a spectator to the argument, eventually throws Coleman out of the game.

Can he do this?

O **ANSWER:** Yes, he can. The home-plate umpire is the umpire-in-chief.

Afterwards, Terry Pendleton, the Braves third baseman and a friend of Coleman's, said, "I don't know why Darling even threw him out. He [Coleman] was arguing with the third-base ump. Darling should have no authority to throw him out."

Only the authority of being the umpire-in-chief.

THE WAY THE BALL BOUNCES

On August 22,1992, Charlie Hayes of the Yankees, with no runners on base in a scoreless tie, hit a pitch by Chuck Finley of the Angels high and far down the left-field line at Yankee Stadium. The ball hit the "wire netting extending along the side of the pole on fair territory above the fence to enable the umpires more accurately to judge fair and foul balls," and rebounded to left fielder Luis Polonia in fair territory.

Did the third-base umpire rule the hit a foul ball, a home run, a double, or a ball that was still in play?

○ **ANSWER:** A home run. Today, the foul poles in all major-league parks are placed in fair territory, behind the fence or wall. Thus, any batted ball that hits either the foul pole or the wire netting extending from it is a home run. *Rule 2.00 A FAIR BALL*

SWINGING THIRD STRIKE

One of the most famous plays in baseball history took place in the bottom of the ninth inning of Game Three of the 1941 World Series. The Brooklyn Dodgers, down to the Yankees 2-1, were leading, 4-3, with two out and no one on base. Tommy Henrich was the batter for New York; Hugh Casey was the pitcher for Brooklyn. The count ran to three-and-two on Henrich. Then Casey broke off a hard curve—some said it was a spitter—and Henrich swung and missed. The game would have been over—but the ball got away from catcher Mickey Owen and rolled back to the screen, as Henrich ran safely to first base.

Then the roof fell in on Brooklyn. Joe DiMaggio singled and Charlie Keller doubled two runs home. After Bill Dickey walked, Joe Gordon doubled two more runs across the plate. The Yankees ended up winning the game, 7-4. When Henrich swung and missed, it appeared that Brooklyn had tied the Series at two games apiece. Instead, the Yankees held a commanding three-game-to-one lead. The next day, the Yankees won 3-1 and wrapped up a Series they very well could have lost.

In retrospect, though, wasn't Henrich's swinging strike the third out of the inning, and the final out of the game?

○ **ANSWER:** No. To conclude a strikeout, the catcher must hold the third strike or pick up the loose ball and throw it to first base before the runner for the out to count. Henrich was safe at first base because he reached it before the throw. *Rule 6.09 (b).*

A NO-WYNN SITUATION

Hal Morris of the Reds is at the plate with one out and a teammate on third base. Before the Pirate pitcher releases his next pitch, he balks, but Morris lines a drive off center fielder Andy Van Slyke's glove for a double. The runner at third starts for home on the play, but when he sees that Van Slyke has a possible play on the ball, he returns to third. When Van Slyke doesn't catch the ball, Morris tags and starts for home again. However, the Pittsburgh outfielder makes a quick recovery and throws to the plate while the runner retreats to third.

Red manager Lou Piniella comes out of the dugout after the play and tells the plate umpire he is waiving the balk call. He wants to take the play instead. But the umpire says he can't.

Why?

○ **ANSWER:** In order for the play to supersede the balk, all runners who were on base had to advance at least one base. *Rule 8.05 (m)* *PENALTY*. The runner at third would score on the balk, but Morris would have to come back to the plate and try all over again.

In April 1977, Jimmy Wynn of the Yankees was the runner at third base, and Lou Piniella was the hitter. Jerry Garvin of the Blue Jays was the pitcher with two out in the bottom of the fourth inning. Piniella "doubled" off the center fielder's glove, but Wynn didn't score on the play. He did score on Garvin's balk, though, while Piniella had to be tossed out of the game before he would give up second base and the double he had hit. Piniella's replacement struck out, and the Yankees went on to lose both the game and their protest.

YOU'VE GOT TO RUN 'EM OUT

In a 1992 game between the White Sox and the host Yankees, New York's Randy Velarde singles to right field, a run scoring on the play. Dan Pasquats relay throw misses the cut-off man, however, and Velarde continues on to second base on the play.

When catcher Carlton Fisk realizes that there is no White Sox teammate backing up the play, he races to retrieve the ball as it rolls toward the visitors' third-base dugout. At the last possible second, he slides feet-first into the dugout in order to stop and recover the ball. Ultimately, he takes firm possession of the ball, which had come to rest on the top step of the dugout.

Velarde, who thinks that the ball has gone into dead territory, and that he is entitled to a free base, trots to third base, but Fisk now steps out of the dugout and throws the ball to third baseman Robin Ventura for an easy tag-out.

The Yankees don't protest the call. Should they have?

○ **ANSWER:** No. A fielder or catcher may reach or step into, or go into, the dugout with one or both feet to make a catch (play), and if he holds the ball, the catch (play) shall be allowed. The ball is in play. *Rule 7.04 (c).*

BALL HITS HELMET

Ivan Calderon, Spike Owen, and Tim Wallach are on third, second, and first bases, respectively, when Gary Carter hits a tailor-made double-play ball to the second baseman. But Wallach, in running from first to second, accidentally loses his batting helmet; the ball hits it and then bounces past the fielder into the outfield while two runs score and Tim advances to third base on the play.

Legal play?

○ **ANSWER:** Yes. In cases where a batting helmet is accidentally hit by a batted or thrown ball, the ball remains in play. It is the same as if the helmet were not hit by the ball. *Rule 6.05 (h).*

Willie Mays, of course, was known for losing his hat while run-

340 ft

"The ball is still in play when it hits a helmet by accdent."

ning the bases. Later, it became mandatory for players, beginning with the 1972 season, to wear a protective batting helmet. While with the Mets, in 1973, in Mays's last major-league season, he lost his helmet in the above situation while running between first and second base. Instead of a double play ensuing, the batter got credited with two runs batted in.

LINES ARE LINES

David Cone is the pitcher for the Mets. Mackey Sasser is the catcher. Cone blows the batter away with a swinging strike on a hard slider that goes down and away, but Sasser has trouble holding onto the pitch and it bounces about five feet to his right.

Since there is no one on base and no out, the batter runs out the play, but in running the last half of the distance from home to first, he runs "outside" of the three-foot line, and Sasser's throw to first baseman Eddie Murray hits him and bounces down the right-field line. The batter goes to second base on the play.

Does he have to give up his base?

○ **ANSWER:** Yes, he is called out because he has interfered with Sasser's throw. The only time a batter can run inside or outside the three-foot line is when he is trying to avoid a fielder trying to play a batted ball. *Rule 6.05 (k).*

A few years back, that same play occurred in a Mariner vs. Yankees game at Yankee Stadium. Don Slaught was the Yank catcher and Don Mattingly was the first baseman. The Seattle batter-runner was called out for interference.

TWO FOR THE PRICE OF ONE

John Kruk of the Phillies hits what appears to be a certain double-play ball to Jose Lind, the Pirates' second baseman. Lind fields the ball cleanly and gives a perfect toss to shortstop Jay Bell, who has enough time to take two full steps to touch second on the right-field side of the base. But before Bell can relay the ball to first for the inning-ending double play, the base runner from first veers deliberately out of his path to take out Bell, preventing him from making the throw.

What's the umpire's call, if any?

○ **ANSWER:** The umpire calls the batter out because of the runner's interference. *Rule 6.05 (m).*

This play has happened thousands of times in the major leagues. Today, the umpires are more likely to penalize the flagrant runner. At one time, it was merely considered part of the game.

In 1949, for example, the Yankees thought that the Red Sox were roughing up their shortstop, Phil Rizzuto. One day, in retaliation, Joe DiMaggio slid directly at Red Sox shortstop Vern Stephens, who was well out of the base path, to break up a double play. Stephens made no throw to first, and the umpire assessed no penalty against DiMaggio and the batter-runner.

DiMaggio's slide had a twofold result: The runner was safe at first and the Red Sox left Rizzuto alone from that day forward.

But today it's different.

A MATTER OF JUDGMENT

In a game at the Oakland Coliseum, Kelly Gruber of the Blue Jays hits a soft pop foul towards the third-box seats. The A's third baseman, Carney Lansford, makes a running catch about 10 feet from the boxes, but his momentum carries him into the wire protecting fence, the ball dropping out of his glove upon contact.

Is it a legal catch?

○ **ANSWER:** It's a matter of judgment on the umpire's part. The rule book says that if the fielder has contact with another fielder or wall immediately following his contact with the ball—and drops it—it is not a legal catch. Ten feet would seem to be a considerable distance, but it wasn't in the following application. *Rule 2.00 CATCH.*

Late in the 1982 season, the host Braves were leading the Padres when San Diego's Gene Richards, with no one on and two out, sent a

"Sorry, folks, but I've got to catch this."

twisting fly ball down the left-field line. Terry Harper made a running catch inside the foul line, but his momentum carried him across the line into the bullpen railing. Trying to cushion his landing, he grabbed the railing but dropped the ball. Umpire Ed Vargo called the play a no-catch, and by the time Harper retrieved the ball and returned it to the infield, Richards had circled the bases. The official scorer ruled the play a four base error, but the league office overruled the scoring, and called the play an inside-the-park home run.

THE BOOTED PLAY

The San Francisco Giants have Willie McGee on second base, Will Clark on first base, and Matt Williams at the plate. While the host Cubs have Dave Smith on in relief, Smith's first pitch to Williams bounces in front of the plate, and off the Bruin backstop's shinguard towards the first-base dugout. McGee and Clark move up a base on the wild pitch. But the Cub catcher, in running down the ball, accidentally kicks it into the Cubs' dugout.

What's the ruling? Is it true that runners can advance only one base on a wild pitch?

O **ANSWER:** Yes, runners may advance only one base on a wild pitch that goes into dead territory. However, if the wild-pitch ball remains on the playing field, and is subsequently kicked or deflected into dead territory, the runners shall be awarded two bases from the position the runners are in at the time of the pitch. *Rule 7.05 (h).* *APPROVED RULING.* McGee scores and Clark advances to third.

Early in the 1992 season, a Yankee catcher inadvertently made the above faux pas.

A VACANT RULE

In this hypothetical case, with two out in the bottom of the ninth inning, the home team Phillies are trailing the Pirates, 7-6. John Kruk is the Philadelphia batter, and Lenny Dykstra the runner at first base.

On the first pitch, from Pittsburgh hurler Doug Drabek, Kruk lifts a high pop foul towards the Phillie dugout. As Pirate first baseman Orlando Merced and catcher Don Slaught converge on the ball, the on-deck batter, Darren Daulton, gets caught in the crossfire.

Merced runs into Daulton and drops the ball. The Pirates demand of the home-plate umpire that Kruk be called out because of offensive interference.

Does the umpire comply with the Pittsburgh request?

O **ANSWER:** According to the language of Rule 7.11, he should, but he probably doesn't. The rule says: "The players, coaches or any member of an offensive team shall vacate any space (including both dugouts) needed by a fielder who is attempting to field a batted or thrown ball.

Penalty: Interference shall be called and the batter or runner on whom the play is being made shall be declared out."

But quite often, the umpires don't interpret Rule 7.11 literally. If they feel that the on-deck batter made a legitimate attempt to get out of the ball's way, they probably won't call offensive interference. In the above example, Kruk would probably get at least one more swing at a pitch.

Baseball Trivia

WHO SAID IT?

Baseball has always produced colorful, funny, and interesting quotes. Some of these lines have worked their way into everyday lingo, and some have even become a part of Americana. Who can forget such bits of wisdom as Satchel Paige's "Don't look back. Something might be gaining on you"?

Now it's your turn to read a quote and to match it up with the person who uttered it. So, get started. (Match-up answers are given at the end of the chapter.)

MATCH-UP: MANAGERS' WORDS

1 Who said, in discussing his team's home park: "When you come to the plate in this ballpark, you're in scoring position"?

2 Who made the egotistical comment "Stay close in the early innings, and I'll think of something"?

3 What diminutive skipper said these fiery words: "I think there should be bad blood between all teams"?

4 What manager, saddled with an inept team, moaned, "Can't anyone here play this game?"

5 Who said, "You don't save a pitcher for tomorrow. Tomorrow it may rain"? Big clue: He's also famous for saying, "Nice guys finish last"—although that wasn't exactly what he said.

6 After suffering through a tough road trip, what Reds manager of 1997 said, "When it rains it pours, and we're in the midst of a monsoon"?

    A Charlie Dressen
    B Don Baylor
    C Earl Weaver
    D Casey Stengel
    E Ray Knight
    F Leo Durocher

MATCH-UP: HUMOR

1 When told his salary was more than the earnings of President Hoover, this man stated, "Oh, yeah? Well, I had a better year than he had."

2 On his disdain for artificial grass, this slugger commented, "If a cow can't eat it, I don't want to play on it."

3 When asked for the highlight of his career, this player responded, "I walked with the bases loaded to drive in the winning run in an intrasquad game in spring training."

4 Although he probably wasn't trying to be humorous, this good ol' country boy once said, "They X-rayed my head and didn't find anything."

5 Speaking of his dislike for hitting in Comiskey Park, this player said, "At Wrigley Field, I feel like King Kong. Here, I feel like Donkey Kong."

A Gary Gaetti
B Bob Uecker
C Babe Ruth
D Dick Allen
E Dizzy Dean

MATCH UP: MORE MANAGERS

1 Even though he'd won a World Series in the 1990s, this manager once muttered, "I'm not sure whether I'd rather be managing or testing bulletproof vests."

2 This man's team was injury plagued in 1989, prompting him to observe, "If World War III broke out, I'd guarantee you we'd win the pennant by 20 games. All our guys would be 4-F. They couldn't pass the physical."

3 In 1997, this White Sox skipper philosophized, "I learned a long time ago, in this game you might as well take the blame because you're going to get it anyway."

4 His pitcher entered the game with the bases loaded. Two wild pitches later, the bases were empty because all three men had scored, leading to this managerial quip: "Well, that's one way to pitch out of a bases-loaded jam." Clue: He was managing the Brewers when this occurred.

    A Terry Bevington
    B Tom Trebelhorn
    C Whitey Herzog
    D Joe Torre

MATCH UP:
LAST CALL FOR MANAGERS' QUOTES

1 Lucky enough to be the manager of George Brett, this man was asked what he told Brett regarding hitting. The Royals manager replied, "I tell him, 'Attaway to hit, George.'"

2 Never known for his use of grammar, this great manager once said of a player's injury, "There's nothing wrong with his shoulder except some pain, and pain don't hurt you."

3 On what it takes to be a successful manager, an all-time big-name manager opined, "A sense of humor and a good bullpen."

4 Two quotes from the same man. A) "I'm not the manager because I'm always right, but I'm always right because I'm the manager." B) "The worst thing about managing is the day you realize you want to win more than your players do."

5 This manager-for-one-day naively believed, "Managing isn't all that difficult. Just score more runs than the other guy."

A Ted Turner   **D** Jim Frey
B Whitey Herzog   **E** Sparky Anderson
C Gene Mauch

MATCH UP: THIS AND THAT

1 Who said: "Baseball statistics are a lot like a girl in a bikini. They show a lot, but not everything"?

2 Two quotes from an ex-catcher: A) "When Steve [Carlton] and I die, we are going to be buried 60 feet, 6 inches apart." B) On Bob Gibson: "He is the luckiest pitcher I ever saw. He always pitched when the other team didn't score any runs."

3 During 1998 spring training, this man came to camp over-weight. He joked, "I must have had five coaches come up to me and say, 'I expected to see you floating over the stadium tied to a string...'"

4 Who was so arrogant that he once proclaimed, "The only rea-son I don't like playing in the World Series is I can't watch myself play"?

5 Soon after being traded, a disgruntled player, asked about the condition of his shoulder, replied, "My shoulder's O.K., but I've still got a scar where the Mets stuck the knife in my back."

A Dante Bichette   **D** Tim McCarver
B Toby Harrah   **E** Reggie Jackson
C Tug McGraw

MATCH UP: MORE THIS AND THAT

1 This manager summarized the futures of two 20-year-old prospects, saying, "In ten years, Ed Kranepool has a chance to be a star. In ten years, Greg Goosen has a chance to be thirty."

2 This Hall-of-Famer said, "So what if I'm ugly? I never saw anyone hit with his face."

3 Tired of being reduced to sitting on the bench, and ignoring his lack of productivity, this man said his team was guilty of the "worst betrayal by a team in all sports history. It's not fair to Deion Sanders. It's not fair to teammates or to the fans, either. It's one of the worst things ever done to a player." P.S.: His team went on to win the World Series without him.

4 After fanning in a two-out, potential game-winning situation in the bottom of the 9th inning, this Pittsburgh Pirate of the past lamented, "It's what you dream of right there, either you're Billy the Kid or Billy the Goat."

A Glenn Wilson
B Casey Stengel
C Deion Sanders
D Yogi Berra

MATCH UP: MORE HUMOR

1 Who said: "I've never played with a pitcher who tried to hit a batter in the head. Most pitchers are like me. If I'm going to hit somebody, I'm going to aim for the bigger parts"?

2 This West Virginia native wasn't too worldly when he broke into the majors. During his ride to Wrigley Field for his first visit there, he spotted Lake Michigan and asked, "What ocean is that?"

3 Who was the player Dante Bichette was referring to when he said: "He's the kid who, when he played Little League, all the parents called the president of the league and said, 'Get him out of there, I don't want him to hurt my son.' I had my mom call the National League office to see if she could do it for me"?

4 What player was former pitcher Darold Knowles talking about when he uttered these words: "There isn't enough mustard in the world to cover him"?

5 Who said: "We live by the Golden Rule—those who have the gold make the rules"?

A Bert Blyleven
B Buzzi Bavasi
C John Kruk
D Mark McGwire
E Reggie Jackson

MATCH UP: COLORFUL QUOTES

1 What American League pitcher said of his first trip to Yankee Stadium, "The first time I ever came into a game there, I got in the bullpen car, and they told me to lock the doors"?

2 This pitcher apparently got tired of being asked trite questions from reporters. Once, after surrendering a home run that cost him a 1-0 defeat, he was asked what it was he had thrown to game hero Tony Conigliaro. The succinct reply was, "It was a baseball."

3 This manager did so well, he was rewarded by the Cardinals. Owner August Busch, who was eighty-five at the time, told the manager he could have a lifetime contract. The St. Louis skipper countered with, "Whose lifetime? Yours or mine?"

4 This colorful character was a fine pitcher. His World Series ledger was golden: 6-0 with a 2.86 ERA. When asked to explain his success, he attributed it to "clean living and a fast outfield."

A Joe Horlen
B Mike Flannagan
C Lefty Gomez
D Whitey Herzog

MATCH UP: FINAL INNING

1 This peppery manager would upstage umpires at the drop of a hat. He even loved to peck umps with the beak of his hat. He offered one of his most famous lines after he showed up the umpires by taking a rule book out on the field. He stated, "There ain't no rule in the rule book about bringing a rule book on the field."

2 This umpire had a rivalry with the manager from the above quote. He once said, "That midget can barely see over the top of the dugout steps, and he claims he can see the pitches."

3 An ex-pitcher, this announcer butchered the English language. In one case, he said a player had "slud into third" instead of "slid." Another remark was, "Don't fail to miss tomorrow's game."

4 After hitting four homers in a game to tie the single-game record, this power hitter said quite correctly, "I had a good week today."

A Earl Weaver
B Marty Springstead
C Dizzy Dean
D Bob Horner

HAS IT EVER HAPPENED?

There are things that have happened in baseball that are incredibly hard to believe. Just imagine: Chicago Cubs outfielder Hack Wilson once actually drove home 191 runs during a single season, and he did it in a mere 155 games. This section tests your knowledge of similarly improbable events.

To keep you honest, every once in a while we'll throw you a wicked curveball, such as a trick question. Then, we'll try to fool you with a change-up in which one of the "facts" in the question will be off by a gnat's eyelash. Your job is to determine the truth and figure out if our events ever really happened.

Potent Lineup

Has a team ever had as many as six players in the lineup drive in 100 or more runs during a season?

ANSWER: No, but the 1936 Yankees featured an incredibly productive lineup with a record five men who had more than 100 ribbies.

The men included three future Hall of Famers: first baseman Lou Gehrig, who amassed 152 RBI; center fielder Joe DiMaggio, who added 125; and catcher Bill Dickey with his 107 RBI. In addition, Tony Lazzeri had 109, and George Selkirk contributed 107.

No-Hit Glory

Has a pitcher ever come up with a no-hitter during his very first start?

O **ANSWER:** Amazingly, the answer is yes. More amazingly, the pitcher wasn't very good at all. Alva "Bobo" Holloman had pitched exclusively out of the bullpen. Then, after begging owner Bill Veeck to give him a start, he came up with his gem back in 1953. Although Holloman succeeded that day, his luck didn't last; he was gone from the majors for good just a short time later that same year.

His career statistics are paltry: 3 wins versus 7 losses, an ERA of 5.23, and twice as many walks (50) as batters struck out. His no-hitter was his only complete game ever.

Fanning Infrequently

Has a major-leaguer gone an entire season while striking out fewer than, say, 25 times?

O **ANSWER:** Not in a long time, but yes, it has been done. In fact, Cleveland's Joe Sewell did this with ease. Sewell was known for his bat control, and, in 1925 and 1929, he truly showcased that talent. During those seasons, he struck out a mere eight times, four each year. Men have been known to strike out four times in a day; it took an entire year for Sewell to do that. Furthermore, he had 608 at bats in 1925 and 578 in 1929.

Impotent Bats

Has there ever been a season in which nobody in the entire American League hit .300 or better? Could such a season of pitchers' domination occur?

O **ANSWER:** Although there was never a season without at least one .300 hitter, there was a year in which only one man topped that level. The year 1968 was known as the "Year of the Pitcher." That season, the American League batting title went to Boston's Carl Yastrzemski, who hit .301. The next best average was a paltry .290. The A.L. pitchers prevailed that year; five of them had ERAs under 2.00.

That was also the season that one of every 5 games resulted in a shutout. It seemed as if every time St. Louis Cardinal Bob Gibson pitched, he tossed a shutout (he had 13). His ERA (1.12) was the fourth lowest in baseball history. Finally, that season also featured the game's last 30-game winner, Detroit's Denny McLain (31-6).

WHO AM I?

1 People stand next to me and realize just how small they are. I'm six-foot-five, weigh about 245 pounds, and have arms as big as some guys' legs. For the most part, I've had my way with pitchers, especially lately. I hit 52 home runs in 1996 and came back in 1997 with 58 long balls. In 1998, I matched that figure by September 2, and then, under the glare of the national spotlight, thrilled the baseball world by adding a dozen more the last three and a half weeks of the season. I cooled off in 1999 and only hit 65 homers. *Who am I?*

2 I have a brother who is an identical twin, but our careers are hardly identical. He played in just 24 games With the A's and Cardinals in the early 1990s. On the other hand, I, who am bulkier than my brother, won the American League MVP in 1988 when I belted 42 home runs, drove in 124 runs, and added 40 stolen bases for good measure. I pounded a league-leading 44 home runs in 1991, but didn't win the MVP. I've been on the disabled list a lot in recent years (seven times since 1993), but still have racked up my share of homers—I hit a career-high 46 in 1998 and slugged 34 in 1999, even though I missed almost one-third of the season. *Who am I?*

3 Stan Musial, Robin Yount, and I are the only players who rank first all-time for a franchise in singles, doubles, triples, and home runs. In my long and distinguished career, I amassed 2035 singles, 665 doubles, 137 triples, and 317 home runs, for a total of 3154 hits, which earned me induction into the Hall of Fame in 1999, the first year that I was eligible. Home run number 200 came off Mitch Williams in his rookie campaign of 1986, after he had been misquoted in my team's local newspaper. The Rangers were coming to town and one of the writers who covered my team asked Mitch how he felt about facing me for the first time, and he answered, "The rumor is that I'm wild and I throw hard, so he might not be too comfortable in there his first at bat." The paper twisted Mitch's words and printed a headline the next day which said that I was scared of Mitch. When I faced Mitch during the series, he threw me a fastball, and I hit it 440 feet over the center field fence for a home run. After the game, the writer commended me on the home run, and I joked, "Yeah, but I was scared doing it." *Who am I?*

4 I had a laundry list of accomplishments. To name a few, I hit a grand slam in my first big league game in 1968, scored 110 or more runs five straight years (1969–73), and hit 25 or more home runs in a season for five different teams, including the Yankees, Angels, and Indians. Believe it or not, I lost my stroke so badly late in my career that I was sent back to the minors. My son has shown no signs of losing his stroke, though—in 1996, he hit his 333rd career home run to pass me, and in 1999, he moved up to 22nd on the all-time home run list, finishing the year with 445. *Who am I?*

5 To win a Rookie of the Year Award, a Cy Young Award, an ERA title, two strikeout titles, fan 16 in a game three times, and pitch on a World Series winner in a career is pretty good—I did all that before I turned 22. Too much success so quickly was kind of hard to handle, and caused me some off-the-field problems and cost me some wins for a few years. Things hit rock bottom in the mid-1990s when I missed most of two seasons, but I got back on track in 1996 when I won 11 games and no-hit Lou Piniella's Mariners. *Who am I?*

6 I have a unique distinction: I'm the only pitcher who has won a Cy Young Award and guest-starred on The Brady Bunch. I won the Cy Young in 1962 when I led major league pitchers with 25 wins and 232 strikeouts. In 1965, I won 23, two less than my teammate Sandy Koufax. In 196S, I set a record—since broken by Orel Hershiser—when I pitched 58⅔ consecutive scoreless innings. And then in 1970, a year after I retired, I gave 15-year-old Greg Brady some tips on pitching. A lot of good it did him— he got a big head and his next game went out and was rocked for 12 runs in the first inning before the manager came out and gave him the hook. *Who am I?*

7 A lot of fans think I'm cocky and a showboat for my antics on the field, but in fact I'm so unpretentious that one year while some of my teammates drove to games in their fancy cars, I rode my bicycle. Here are a few tidbits about my career: I was originally drafted by the Royals, but first played for the Yankees. I led the National League in triples with 14 in 1992. I stole 56 bases for the Reds in 1997 to finish second to Tony Womack. Finally— and I don't mean to sound cocky— I'm the only man who has played in both a World Series and a Super Bowl. *Who am I?*

8 Every time I turned around in 1973, some pro sports team was drafting me. The Padres selected me in the first round of the baseball draft (I was first-team All-American my senior year as a pitcher tout fielder for the University of Minnesota), the NBA's Atlanta Hawks and ABA's Utah Jazz chose me in the fifth and sixth rounds, respectively, and even though I didn't play football in college, the Minnesota Vikings picked me in the 17th round of the NFL draft. In between signing with the Padres in 1973 and stroking my 3000th hit for the Twins in 1993, I hit 25 or more home runs nine times, drove in 100 runs eight times, and feuded with George Steinbrenner almost as much as Reggie and Billy. *Who am I?*

9 1982 was a pretty good year for me: I was voted one of the 10 best casually dressed men in America, and my Cardinals team won the World Series. Other notables on the best dressed list included Alexander Haig and Johnny Carson. As a matter of fact, Johnny hosted The Tonight Show in Burbank, not far from where I grew up and went to Locke High School in Los Angeles. By coincidence, Lonnie Smith, one of the guys I played ball with as a teenager in L.A., was a teammate on my 1982 team. Lonnie had a long career in the majors—17 years—but I played 19 years. I only hit 28 home runs in those 19 seasons, and my lifetime average was less than .270, but my friends tell me I'll probably be voted into the Hall of Fame; I'll be up for induction in 2002. *Who am I?*

10 Major league scouts weren't exactly beating a path to my door when I was playing high school ball for Phoenixville High, outside Philadelphia—I was picked in the 62nd round (the 1389th player) of the 1988 draft. I hung in there, though, made it to the majors, and after the 1998 season I signed a longterm contract for mega-millions. What did I do to justify that mammoth contract? I averaged .335, 33 home runs, and 106 RBIs a year over the previous six seasons, playing a position where guys usually hit .260 with half that many homers and runs batted in. I owe a lot to my godfather, who turned out to be my manager for the first four years of my major league career. *Who am I?*

11 We couldn't have written a baseball quiz book without including one question on "The Bambino" himself, George Herman "Babe" Ruth. Here are 10 statements about the Babe. We want to know if they're true or false.

A He stole more than 100 bases in his career.
B He finished his career with the Boston Braves.
C He was born in New York and died in Baltimore.
D He was a 20-game winner for the Red Sox.

E His career average was higher than teammate Lou Gehrig's.

F He is the all-time career leader in RBIs.

G He holds the American League record for most strikeouts in a season by a batter.

H He was six feet, two inches tall.

I He hit .400 in a season once.

J He didn't drink, smoke, or carouse.

12 From the late 1940s until the early 1980s, there were three sure things in life: death, taxes, and this colorful character going to the World Series. Over a 35-year period (1947–81), he suited up for 21 Fall Classics: 14 as a player, five as a coach, and two as a manager, and his team came out on the long end of the stick 13 times. One final hint, which should clinch it for you. The story has it that one time he went to pick up a pizza for one and was asked whether he wanted it cut in four or eight slices. "You better make it four," he said, "I could never eat eight."

13 All right, quick now, name the only two players who started their careers in 1975 or later who collected at least 3250 hits. We'll add that they combined for 738 home runs and 614 stolen bases.

14 The Yankees closed out the century in a grand fashion. In 1998, they set an American League record with 114 regular-season wins and then swept the Rangers in the Division Series, beat the Indians four games to two in the League Championship Series, and swept the Padres in the World Series. Their two losses in the post-season was the fewest since the three-tier post-season system was first used in 1995. In 1999, the Yankees were less of a juggernaut during the season as they won 98 games, but they were even more dominating in the post-season. They again swept the Rangers in the Division Series, beat the Red Sox four games to one in the League Championship Series, and whitewashed the Braves in the World Series; thus, the 1999 Yankees lost only one game in the postseason. From 1969 to 1993, when baseball utilized two post-season rounds (there were three rounds in the strike-shortened 1981 season), only one team went undefeated by sweeping both the League Championship Series and the World Series. *Who was it?*

15 Every dog has his day, and every star doesn't always shine. Hank Aaron is the all-time home run leader, Cal Ripken Jr. holds the iron-man streak, and Brooks Robinson set some records with his amazing defense at third base. But Aaron, Ripken, and Robinson, along with Mickey Mantle and Reggie Jackson, each hold at least one record that they would just as soon not. Match the player with the record.

Hank Aaron	**A** Holds record for most strikeouts in World Series play
Cal Ripken Jr.	**B** The mark for most double plays grounded into in a career belongs to him
Brooks Robinson	**C** Set record for most at bats in a season without a triple
Reggie Jackson	**D** Hit into a record four triple plays
Mickey Mantle	**E** All-time leader in lifetime K's 70

16 What's more exciting, watching Juan Gonzalez or Manny Ramirez go deep, or seeing Kenny Lofton or Tony Womack steal second on a bang-bang play? Because we already have a lot of questions on home run hitters, we're going to ask you about some great base stealers. These would be hanging curvebals if we asked you who the top three all-time base thieves are (Rickey Henderson, Lou Brock, and Ty Cobb; you knew that, right?), so try to answer these questions about four other players in the top 15.

A This shortstop stole 104 bases for the Dodgers in 1962 to set the single-season record, which Brock broke in 1974.

B Starting in 1985, he won six straight stolen base titles for the Cardinals, averaging 92 per year with three 100-steal seasons. He's fifth on the career list with 762.

C He's first among players who never won a stolen base title, with 689 steals.

D This outfielder pilfered 668 bases, most of them for the Royals in the late 1970s and 1980s.

17 The first 80 years of the 20th century, perfect games were a rare commodity—only eight pitchers twirled perfectos. But the hurlers picked up the pace over the last two decades by throwing seven—or one approximately every three years. All good pitchers in the group, but it's unlikely that any will go to the Hall. We've given you the year and the team for whom each of the seven pitched the gem.

YEAR	TEAM	YEAR	TEAM
1981	Cleveland Indians	1994	Texas Rangers
1984	California Angels	1998	New York Yankees
1988	Cincinnati Reds	1999	New York Yankees
1991	Montreal Expos		

18 In 1999, Sammy Sosa led his Cubs team in home runs for the seventh consecutive season. Impressive stretch by Slammin' Sammy, but a long way from the record. In the first half of the century, a player led his team—the same team—in home runs 18 consecutive seasons. Seven of those seasons, he had at least twice as many homers as the number-two man on the team. He averaged about 28 per year over the 18-year period. He managed the team the last four years. Any idea who it is?

19 Isn't it about time some player won the Triple Crown? After all it's been more than 30 years—since 1967—when a player led his league with a .326 average, 44 home runs, and 121 RBIs. These were the only home run and RBI titles this player won in his long and accomplished career, but he also won batting titles in 1963 and 1968. He's second to Pete Rose on the all-time games played list with 3308, seventh in career hits with 3419, and 11th in lifetime RBIs with 1844. Can you name him?

20 Name the team: They have only been to one World Series since 1919 and they lost. Luke Appling is their all-time hit leader. Ted Lyons is their all-time wins leader. Nellie Fox won the MVP for them in 1959. Tommie Agee won the Rookie of the Year for them in 1966. Jeff Torborg and Jim Fregosi have managed the team. If we told you much more, we'd give it away.

ANSWERS

Managers' Words:

1 B

2 A

3 C

4 D

5 F

6 E

Humor: 1 C   2 D   3 B   4 E   5 A

More Managers: 1 D   2 C   3 A   4 B

Last Call for Managers' Quotes: 1 D   2 E   3 B   4 C   5 A

This and That: 1 B   2 D   3 A   4 E   5 C

More This and That: 1 B   2 D   3 C   4 A

More Humor: 1 A   2 C   3 D   4 E   5 B

Colorful Quotes: 1 B   2 A   3 D   4 C

Final Inning: 1 A   2 B   3 C

Who Am I?

1 Mark McGwire

2 Jose Canseco

3 George Brett

4 Bobby Bonds

5 Dwight Gooden

6 Don Drysdale

7 Deion Sanders

8 Dave Winfield

9 Ozzie Smith

10 Mike Piazza

11 **A** True   **B** False   **C** False   **D** True   **E** True   **F** False
   G False   **H** True   **I** False   **J** False

12 Yogi Berra (14 as a player for the Yankees, four as a coach of
   the Yankees, one as a coach of the Mets, one as a manager of
   the Mets and one as a manager of the Yankees.)

13 Paul Molitor (3319 hits, 234 home runs, and 504 stolen
   bases) and Eddie Murray (3255 hits, 504 home runs, and 110
   stolen bases.)

14 The 1976 Reds; they swept the Phillies in the League
   Championship Series and the Yankees in the World Series

15 Aaron–**B** (328   Ripken–**C** (646 in 1989)   Robinson–**D**;
   Jackson **E** (2597)   Mantle: **A** (54)

16 **A** Muary Wills   **B** Vince Coleman   **C** Joe Morgan   **D** Willie
   Wilson

17 Len barker (Indians), Mike Witt (Angles), Tom Browning
   (Reds), Dennis Martinez (Expos), Kenny rogers(Rangers),
   David Wells (1998 Yankees), and David Cone (1999 Yankees).

18 Mel Ott (New York Giants)

19 Carl Yastrzemski

20 Chicago White Sox

Roster